Praise for The *Female Rogue: A Memoir of Living Fiercely*

"A beautiful writer, a shaper of words and dreams. The whimsy and logic and history, both personal and book-learned, take my breath away. You have a winner here."

—Susan Fifer Canby, Vice President Emeritus,
National Geographic Society

"Both brilliant and embodied, Jackson has a voice that's desperately needed and instantly relatable. Jackson's work is so critical to add to the growing chorus that believes as she does—that actually it's good to be human, innately good; from soul to skin, from bones to breath."

—Meggan Watterson, MDIV, MTS, feminist theologian and *Wall Street Journal* best-selling author of *Mary Magdalene Revealed*

"Jacquelyn Jackson's memoir offers a full-throated, fully human, fully divine voice that brings to life the opportunity to reclaim the truth of our beauty."

—Jeanne Marie Mudd, Founder and CEO, Watershed Ways

THE FEMALE ROGUE

THE FEMALE ROGUE

A Memoir of Living Fiercely

Jacquelyn L. Jackson

SWP

SHE WRITES PRESS

Published in 2025 by

She Writes Press, an imprint of The Stable Book Group

32 Court Street, Suite 2109

Brooklyn, NY 11201

https://shewritespress.com

Library of Congress Control Number: 2025913085

ISBN: 979-8-89636-012-4

eISBN: 979-8-89636-013-1

Interior Designer: Kiran Spees

Printed in the United States

Names and identifying characteristics have been changed to protect the privacy of certain individuals.

For female rogues everywhere
who strive to be seen, felt, and lived.

Contents

PROLOGUE

FIELDS OF GRAPES, lavender, sunflowers, and stunning hilltop vistas welcome us to the Villa La Selva Giardino del Belvedere in Tuscany's Chianti Hills. My husband and I join four other couples for two weeks at the stone villa that sits amidst groves of ancient oaks, olive trees just beginning to fruit, and an azure saltwater pool to ease our travel-weary bodies.

Montevarchi, an ancient town that dates to 1100 CE, is a 2.7-kilometer slow wind down the hill. The town has a co-op supermarket for groceries and a train station that can transport us to Florence in less than an hour.

The first two days of our early September visit, we laze at the villa, sip chianti, and spend long hours in the saltwater pool. On day three, we hop the train to Florence, a city I have yearned to visit for many years.

We have a tour guide for the Uffizi Gallery and the Accademia Gallery where Michelangelo's *David* holds court. Our guide leads us through narrow, gently crowded cobblestoned streets. The wicked heat of July and August has abated, and I breathe a contented sigh as I soak in ancient architecture, the aroma of roasted garlic and leather goods, and offerings of gelato, Tuscan ceramics, and stationery.

A flash of hot pink from a shop window catches my eye. I linger a moment and realize I am looking at refrigerator magnets shaped like penises. Really? Are they tacky souvenirs of Michelangelo's statue? No idea. But a few more steps and I stumble on the real thing. A thirty-something man sits on the narrow sidewalk, legs spread wide, his feet in the street as he examines his fully exposed penis. I gawk.

Hot pink and flesh-and-blood penises are harbingers of what awaits us in Florence. The city offers a panoply of masculine imagery in two and three dimensions. Cathedrals and galleries are hung with works by renowned artists who drew inspiration and funding from the Catholic Church and rich-ruling families. The penis reigns supreme in Florence.

The Biblical commandment—*Thou shalt not make unto thee any graven image*—was ignored by early church leaders. Graven images abound. The vast majority are of men or by men while female renderings, primarily by male artists, are much less prevalent and primarily depict virgins and vulnerability: the Virgin Mary, a queen or two, and re-creations of the rape and kidnapping of young, often naked, females.

I feel suffocated by the male gaze. Where are the female artists? How about images of rowdy and defiant girls and women? Why no females unbound by sexualization, virginity, or motherhood? The sheer force of female erasure lands like a direct punch to my belly. Patriarchy is deified by every artistic medium while female agency, both sacred and profane, has been erased.

As we wander the Uffizi, our guide explains the male faces sketched into the corners of many framed masterpieces. The artists, she tells us, painted themselves into the actual pictures, claiming their place beside popes and kings.

"Those are self-portraits," our guide explains. "It is just like branding today!"

My skin feels branded by history and encaged by masculine celebrations of male divinity and violent conquer. As I wander, I suddenly feel the eyes of all the sexualized and subservient females, hung on walls and trapped in oil and clay, staring at me. Their fierce collective gaze pierces my body.

I swear I hear them plead: *Be all that we could never be.*

As soon as the tour ends, I flee the marbled halls for the blue of a Tuscan afternoon. Leaning against a wall, I bend over a moment gulping in air, trying to calm myself. My breath slows as warm sun bakes into my back, but my insides roil with the pleas of all those female eyes which urged me to go rogue, take every path they were forbidden to trod.

I have ping-ponged throughout my life between cultural obedience and defiance. Roguish at times; sweet-smiling too often. The ancient eyes—*insistent, urgent*—are tired of waiting. I can feel rogue energy bubbling inside of me, loudmouthed and defiant.

I also know and trust my body. As a yoga practitioner for twenty-five years and an instructor for ten, I understand, and have benefited from, the healing power of breath and movement. My body brilliantly guided me through horrific trauma after I witnessed, up close, the murder and wounding of my colleagues and friends, including Congresswoman Gabrielle Giffords, when a bullet penetrated her brain. Eleven months later, my soulmate brother, a tall, thin, organic-eating chiropractor in Austin, Texas, collapsed two weeks after running a 10K, fell into a seven-day coma, and died of an undetected brain tumor.

The combined wallop of the shooting and my brother's death smothered me in grief and trauma. My choice was to respond to my body's shallow breath, pulsing heart, and pitching stomach. Or die. Movement, sweat, focused breath, and guided imagery saved my life.

My body tells truth which over the years I have trusted or over-ridden. On this beautiful late-summer Florence morning, I trust my body. The panic attack convinces me of an undeniable truth: My female DNA carries the genetic mark of centuries-long abuse and erasure.

Enough, the eyes tell me. Enough hot pink and white marble penises. Enough male gods, kings, and generals plastered and painted and held most holy. I cannot erase thousands of years of masculine imagery and mindset, but I can release the trauma of female erasure from my body. Victimhood be damned.

When we return to the villa, I dive into the saltwater pool and swim lap after lap—blood pumping and muscles burning. My genes have been imprinted by centuries of female erasure but I know, first-hand, sweat and breath are powerful change agents.

I flip to my back, peer into the vast cloudless sky and feel myself reflected and affirmed by the natural beauty. An olive tree at the pool's edge has sprouted a host of newborn fruit. Small and soft green. New life. I dunk my head, baptize myself, then leap into the air whooping shouts of joy into the Tuscan sky. Defiant joy.

Two months after our trip to Italy, I have a vivid dream where I search desperately for my rogue. *Where is my rogue? Where is she hidden? Where has she gone?* I trek down steep cliffs and up high mountains. I wander the sidewalks of New York City and a meadow in Montana.

My rogue, my rogue. Where is my rogue? I ask again and again.

When I awaken, I know the female eyes in the Uffizi were urging me to find my rogue, live my rogue. Their eyes penetrated oil and clay to latch onto my body and they were not going to let me go. My dream assures me the Uffizi eyes demand I go rogue. *Live your rogue.* My dream makes clear I am not moving fast enough. I desperately need my rogue. The world desperately needs the rogue of every woman and girl.

A word about rogue. Negative definitions include "unprincipled" and "dishonest, scoundrel, and scamp." But place a "go" in front of "rogue" and you find an energy that strains at its tethers, eager to inspire female lives in an "independent or uncontrolled way that is not authorized, normal, or expected." Female rogues forge a different path than male rogues.

◉

True female rogue energy, my dream assures me, works from the inside out. We swim in a cultural milieu that insists females judge, disdain, fix, and overrule their bodies. The rogue vision: Every inch of female existence is unbound, beautiful, and lived. Female rogues embody fierce resilience, fierce hearts, and fierce determination. My own body shimmered and shook in the Uffizi with the truth of this vision, but it took my rogue dream to kick my butt before I would listen and act.

Go rogue. Claim unauthorized, abnormal, and unexpected. Rogue is the energy that stirs DNA with new messaging. Rogue is imagination that veers outside the lines and blurs delineations of time into a seamless fount of wisdom. Rogue breaks open stereotypes, smashes the chains of creed, dictates, and laws. Rogue opens paths toward health and strength on this earthly plane. Rogue stiches female sexuality, sensuality, and sacredness into a beautiful whole.

Go deep. Body-deep. DNA deep. Here's what I know for certain: Nothing I do in my body will alter my DNA, but roguish behavior can change how my body reads DNA messaging. Acceptance of long-held norms freezes genes into silence, while going rogue unburies truth hidden beneath the silence.

The best news: Neither the DNA inherited ancestrally nor from my family of origin is the boss of me.

Movement, breath, and expanded awareness trigger life-changing biochemical messages through a process called methylation, an epigenetic mark, which means genes can become more or less sensitive to messages from the body.

Read that again.

Methylation is soul and salvation. My body is both a powerful machine and an intuitive creature of imagination and instinct, and I control the levers that send different messaging to my DNA. This I know. My methylation-moment in the Uffizi told me so.

I knew my rogue intimately as a child. I want and need her back, and the female eyes assure me my rogue is alive and well inside me. *Wake up,* their eyes urge, *or you too will remain shellacked in oil and clay.*

My genes and I say yes.

IN THE BEGINNING

When the lips are silent, the heart has a thousand tongues.

—Rumi

MYSTERY AND DIVINITY spin me in my mother's womb from egg to fetus to human. A saltwater world where I swim, wiggle, and kick as divine spirit sanctifies my place in the vast sea of being. Innate certainty guides my journey to human. My cells know the hard work of transformation, and I jump on board for the ride.

The Lego blocks that shape me into human form include about twenty thousand genes, the sections of DNA (deoxyribonucleic acid) that are found inside every human cell. DNA is formed by four chemicals that pair up into a host of combinations that are the codes that make my eyes green, hair brown, and nudge my teeth into a slight overbite.

Gender is nowhere to be seen during this fraught-frenzy of combining. Inside each cell, DNA is tightly wrapped in structures called chromosomes. Every normal cell has twenty-three pairs of chromosomes that are identical in males and females. Except for one: An errant Y chromosome determines whether I face the world as male or female. For about six to seven weeks after sperm and egg meet and swipe right, before the big X or Y reveal, the gonads of my fetus remain undifferentiated. More simply stated: All fetal genitalia are, in the beginning, the same, which means all female-and-male-human-wannabes are on a level playing field.

Until. The playing field tips dramatically when the Y chromosome, present only in males, wakes up late in the second month and grows balls. If two Xs join forces, my genitalia is tucked neatly inside my body.

One fact that excites: My heart comes into being during the six-to-seven-week window of gender-free existence. Just three weeks in, my heart begins to take shape near my brain. A host of growing, folding, and expanding nudges my heart downward through my soon-to-be throat to its resting place in my chest where it is fully formed by week ten.

I am not a scientist and have no authority in this area, but I take great joy in the notion that wisdom, free of gender bias, infused my heart before it folded its way through brain and voice box and landed in my chest.

The remainder of the nine months I swim in my mother's pear-shaped womb, immersed in divine mystery, as roguishly wild as I please. I thrive in the womb's hollowed, hallowed space, fed by an umbilical connection to my mother that fattens me with holy.

In this Eden, I breathe my mother, my mother breathes me. Spirit breathes us both. World without end. Amen.

Of course, I remember my nine months in the womb's rogue-wildland. Womb-time memories shimmer through my every cell, and no one can take from me the sensations of safe and wild swimming through space-time that permeated and grew my blood and bone.

My Eden comes to an abrupt end when harsh white light, cold silvery steel, and pains of labor crash around me like lightning on an angry sea. My umbilical connection is severed; my wet-breath tenure ends. I arrive covered in blood, sweat, viscosity, my hallowed space an empty tomb, my lungs sprung to life as I suck and howl my first tastes of air.

It's a girl, I must have heard myself proclaimed as frothy-pink limitations and expectations lay claim to my body. *It's a girl,* they tell my heavily sedated mother, standard procedure for women giving birth in the 1950s, unheard also by my father who is banished to the waiting room.

My severed umbilical cord staunches the flow of divinity that breathed me in the womb. My skin, puckered by my liquid hollow, air-prickles into a host of goose bumps that rise from me like grasping, needy hands.

I want more, is what I would have said if I had words. More liquid free-floating through time and space. More rogue freedom.

The Earth I land on says no.

Dear Mommy,

My body was severed from yours at birth, but my first conscious awareness of our separation imprints when I am three and a half. You place me on the pine green bathroom rug when you shower to keep an eye on me while I play with my favorite wooden blocks etched with farm animal shapes: a yellow cow, blue pig, and red goat. I look up as you step out of the tub, breathing you in from my knee-high vista.

You are lemon soap, dark hair, olive skin. I feel the soft nub of the rug on my chubby toddler thighs and watch drops of water run down your arms. You are tall and angular with skin taut across the huge curve of your belly that holds what will be my twin brothers. You are swollen breasts tipped by deep-rose cylindrical nipples and a thick black triangle of pubic hair.

Take, feel. Your skin whispers to me of the nine months I spent inside of you. Soul whispers that forever remind me where I began, fed by your marrow, strung together belly-to-belly, blood-to-blood, swimming safe and secure in your salt-water world.

Take, eat. You are my body and blood. Skin is our connection and touch our language. My hunger for you is primal, but I am forced to settle for less after two new baby brothers drop from your body, take my place at your breast.

You slowly towel yourself dry as I memorize your slope and curve. You slip into your worn plaid robe and scoop me into your arms where I rest atop your huge belly and breathe in talcum powder, soft skin. The warmth of your breath on my neck invites me to lean my head against your chest. You are mine for the moment. My body sinks into yours as the strong beat of your heart against my cheek blends us as one. We are a prayer my heart never forgets.

Dear Daddy,

You are other.

My body did not ripen inside of you. I never fed from you, but, still, I know I am of you. Your cheekbones and smile reflect back to me when I look in the mirror. Your sparkly blue eyes and thin brown hair, your twinkle and laugh and love of life and talking, always talking to others. A salesman, natural born and good at it. You sell me on the notion of Father Knows Best. Not with words but with actions that lay the groundwork for me to accept the cultural insistence that male others exert innate power over me.

You are strong arms and prickly whiskers rubbed against

my little-girl cheeks. You are legs and feet that root into my belly as you lay on the living room floor. One foot, two foot supporting my body, swinging me up in the air. "You are flying," you shout, great glee in your voice as you move me side-to-side, back-and-forth, your back on the carpet and me sailing through the air, beaming down on you, giggling from my air perch on your legs, flying high while firmly planted, my belly to your solid feet, loving the ride.

You are the smell of the sweet cut grass you mow on Saturday mornings, Old Spice cologne, and newly sawed wood. You are the yellow of eggs we called "smear arounds" when you let me, so many mornings, swirl my toast through your broken yoke, finger-painting bright yellow on the plate. You are coffee breath, morning toast, butter dripping off slices of browned bread. You are the cigarette butts that you stub out in the broken yellow yolks, and the ride-downs you offer each morning when you have to leave for work and let my older brother and me stand on the running board of our Ford as you slowly back down the driveway toward the street. We hang on with all we have, giggling and thrilled by our magic coach ride.

On special days, you take me with you to business meetings in Victorville, CA, just up the mountain from our home in San Bernardino. Just the two of us, and I love the free time away from my siblings. I sit in the passenger seat as we drive up Cajon Pass, steep and crawling, into the upper desert where sage scrub and yucca trees add touches of green to the dirt brown landscape.

At your favorite Victorville coffee shop, you introduce me as your daughter. I am proud to sit beside you and you order me a chocolate coke all sweet and sugary that I sip slowly through my straw. My legs in the booth do not reach the floor, and I bang my patent leather shoes against the back of the booth, once and again, and you say please stop and I suck through my straw and say, of course, not realizing I am banging nervous-happy-jitters in being, just me, with my father.

We drive back to our house in the San Bernardino Valley, sixty miles east of Los Angeles. As the sun sets you sing an old Army song in your soft tenor, "'Twas only an old beer bottle, sailing in the foam." I know that memory has hijacked you to a place far away from me, next to you in the front seat with the glow of dashboard lights on our faces. "'Twas only an old beer bottle, far away from home."

Mom and I curl together on the couch in the den. Early morning, sky still dark, house hushed as the rest of our family sleeps. I sit beside her, my legs beneath me, hip-to-hip, my head curled toward her shoulder. In the silence of early morning, before birdsong or breakfast bustle, I nestle into her, soak in her warmth, sync my breath with hers. My eleven-year-old body relaxes into the safety of her in our sacred place, body-to-body, blanketed by the silent house.

"I had that dream again," I tell her in my early morning voice.

"Tell me."

Tell me. Two words that form the most enduring gift Mom gives me. An invitation. An initiation. Trust what your dreams tell you. It's your soul talking. Her respect for dreams lands in my heart like a love letter. *Tell me,* she whispers, gifting me belief and reverence. A holy practice born of those early mornings when Mom creates sacred space—no need for altars or statues—just a rust-colored couch, coffee-stained and frayed on one arm. Our sacred space where dreams are cherished, trusted. Her rogue-reverence for dreams frees me of time-space limitations, urges me to trust what I see. I am cinematographer and director of wisdom and creativity, divinity and belief, mom insists.

Every. Single. Night.

"I was in a big empty warehouse," I whisper. "It was dark and cold and my footsteps sounded loud on the cement floor. I was in the middle of the building, walking slow but there was a big hole in the floor and I fell through. I kept dropping and dropping until I finally hit a mattress. I didn't die."

"Were you scared?" Mom asks.

"I was. I hate falling, and I kept falling for a long time."

"Look at that," Mom says to me. "The mattress was there for you. You landed fine. Seems the dream is saying to trust. You might fall but you will be okay."

"Did you look for your big lion?" she asks, knowing well my recurring dream of a friendly lion, golden maned, giant paws, gentle of heart who would slowly turn over when I was frightened to take my fear away.

"He came," I say as I sink deeper into the warmth of Mom's arms. "He rolled over and I was okay." My sense of safety in the dream leaks through the morning quiet and into the warm snuggle of my mother.

Mom neither lectures nor preaches. She invites me to pay attention, to believe what I know to be true. Create quiet spaces. Listen to and trust inner voices of wisdom. An enduring legacy she gifted me, my sister, and our nieces. A profound belief in mystery born of our matrilineal line. *Go rogue.*

◉

My mother sits at the dining room table with our neighbor Frances, who comes over most mornings to share coffee and cigarettes. Frances and Hal live two doors down and have a daughter a year older than me. I am twelve and lie on the living room floor pretending to read as I watch their every move.

Mom sits at one end of the table, her tan legs curled beneath her. She's barefoot and wears Bermuda shorts and a white sleeveless blouse. She tips her head to the side, tilts her chin up, and takes a long, slow drag on her cigarette. White puffs of smoke curl around her dark hair as she slowly, all-the-time-in-the-world, exhales.

The vacuum cleaner idles near the sofa. The washing machine signals it is done. Breakfast dishes sit unrinsed in the sink. Mom and Frances pay no attention. This is their time, their moment. They have transcended the bounds of wife and mother, two free-floating female friends, sitting, only sitting, enjoying each other on a quiet morning.

I cannot hear their words but memorize the body language. Frances laughs like a bawdy sailor and has a husky cigarette voice. My mother, more feminine, almost flirty, lilts her head back as she laughs. Her smile as wide as the Amarillo, Texas, land that grew her. She refills their coffee cups.

Frances is the rogue of the neighborhood mothers. She wears slacks not dresses. She leans back in her chair, arms spread atop the chair, knees akimbo, ankles loosely crossed. Her laugh bursts from her, bounces off the ceiling. She flicks an ash toward the ashtray but misses. Neither woman reaches to brush the ashes away.

In church, there are few graven images of virgins and mothers, and I hunger for different versions of how to be female. Mom and Frances deliver. In my imagination, I paint my mom's lips and nails scarlet, dress her in a flowing red silk gown. She is glamour and mystery to Frances's artistic and boisterous. I memorize their every gesture and giggle.

◉

A long row of tongues protrude from our twelve-year-old mouths as we kneel in a straight row at the altar. The boys wear dark suits and the girls a rainbow of pastel shades of dotted-Swiss half-domed by petticoats. We look like bowls of sherbet. Easter Sunday, 1962, Del Rosa Methodist Church. San Bernardino, California. I am the lime-green scoop on the right.

"Take, eat," Reverend Colette repeats softly as he moves slowly in front of us, placing hard-kernelled rectangles on our eager tongues. "This is the body of Christ who died for you." Reverend Colette's baritone lulls me trancelike: take, eat; take, eat; take, eat.

A good little Methodist, I had studied for this day and was eager for a bite of Christ and a swig of blood. My twelve-year-old bones quiver expectantly as petticoats scratch red marks on my holy little thighs and a plastic lime-green headband bites into my skull.

Reverend Colette places the small rectangle in my mouth. I feel the warmth of his hand and notice dark hair on his knuckles. The kernel glues itself to my tongue. I dare not disturb the body of Christ but I do say a silent prayer that it might soften up a bit. I wait for a holy bolt of lightning from Christ's body, but nothing comes so I nudge the kernel with my tongue, bite down, and swallow.

"Take, drink," Reverend Colette comes down the row again. "This is my blood that was shed for you." He carries tiny glasses of blood in a round metal holder that clanks as he walks. I drink down the blood and the taste slowly registers in my brain.

"Grape juice," I gasp to myself, "and not even Welch's."

I close my eyes and bow my head, trying to look holy, but inside I am reeling. Store-brand grape juice. I tasted Welch's grape juice at my neighbor's house and it is much grapier than the store brand we drink at home.

Wasn't Jesus worth the price of Welch's?

When we get home from church, I bolt from the car and beeline for my bedroom. I strip off pastel and petticoats, unbuckle and fling patent leather shoes and white socks, yank that hard plastic out of my hair, and pull on my Bermuda shorts.

I need the arms of my precious elm tree. Large and welcoming, my umbilical connection to nature. I clamber up and find a sturdy top branch where I lean back and stretch out both legs.

"Hey," I whisper even though no one is around to hear. Just me and my tree.

"Hey, little one," my tree answers in my wide-ranging imagination. I feel the scrape of her bark on my back and along my legs. My mother-tree. My safe place. I sink back into her arms. A cool breeze tickles my legs with shimmery leaves.

"I failed communion," I whisper. "I didn't do it right, I guess. I stuck out my tongue and did everything they said. Do you know: There's no real blood? Just grape juice. Cheap grape juice. I probably wasn't supposed to notice. I guess I messed up."

"You are perfect," my tree tells me with the gentle sway of her branches. She loves my stained Bermuda shorts and the way my hair fights itself free from rubber bands and plastic headbands. She is wood, raw and organic, not yet smoothed and shellacked into hard pews. Her open-armed branches welcome me home, wrap me in sap-running, bark-biting, limb-swinging love. All of me. Just as I am. My elm is queen of rogue-heaven, and I roam and romp through her branches never fearing I might fall. She would not let me.

My parents planted the elm when I was six months old in the exact center of our yard when our one-story stucco subdivision in

San Bernardino was brand new. Built atop what had been an orange grove where not a single orange tree was spared.

The elm and I grew up together, and I took to climbing into her branches as soon as my arms and legs could shimmy up the rough bark, hook my leg over the lowest branch, and pull myself up. In her sea of green, I love to draw my eyes into narrow slits, blending me with green leaves, cool breezes, rough wood, and blue sky.

On my communion Sunday, I climb higher, my heart pumping, sweat dripping, hair free of the rubber band. I skin one knee on the way up and droplets of blood dot my skin. I rub the blood with my index finger and lick my finger clean. Warm and metallic. My body. My blood.

"Take, drink," I say to myself as goose bumps of grace splash my skin. I feel God more alive in leaves and sap than on hard pews. On this day, quivering in communion with my tree, memories of grape juice vanish as the tree tickles me happy.

Dear Rogue,

I wish I had known you were going away. We had each other for twelve years. A natural fit. We stuck together even though church and culture kept trying to pull you away from me, groom me to be obedient, virginal, and sweet.

Over those twelve years, I carried inside every egg that was with me in the womb. Eggs born of my mother's body that were planted inside of her by her mother's body. I imagine a long line of eggs holding hands through time, roosting in the warm wombs of daughter, mother, grandmother, and all the mother-greats. Binding and beautiful. Rogue-eggs, simple and true.

You, sweet rogue, lived easy and natural in my child body.

In those days, my body was more plank than curve, and I knew nothing about how much I weighed. You taught me to eat when I was hungry and stop when full. You climbed me into trees, ran my legs hard and fast through the back alley, skinned my knees and pumped my heart. You insisted I love my body's strength and sweat—every ounce of it every single day. With you alive inside me, I cared not a whit about what I looked like or what others thought.

I had no clue how profoundly my morphing body would change my world. Never guessed, wonder-rogue, you would be suctioned out and away, banished and tamed along with the eggs I was born with that dropped each month from my body. Slow drips of blood that washed you and my eggs away. One, then another, then another.

You shot me full of piss and vinegar, sweat and spit, and saved me from pink-spun webs that liked me dainty and sweet. The world insisted I shove you aside just when I needed you most.

JUDGMENT

Let today be the day you stop living within the confines
of how others define or judge you. You have a unique
beauty and purpose; live accordingly.

—Dr. Steve Maraboli

HORMONES CLAIM MY BODY as I stand by. Helpless. Deft hands that pop out my breasts, carve my waist, plump my hips. And blood. This is not a bloodless coup but comes instead with washes of pain and blood that yank me out of my childhood world where I imagine myself invisible, blended into my elm, oblivious to adult eyes even though they watch over me.

Estrogen comes attached with what feels like a thousand eyes that latch onto my body: strangers' eyes, boys' eyes, and the always-comparing eyes of girls. I am an event at the Olympics: *Look at the sweet curve of that waist. Check out those breasts. Ah, sweet hips. Her hair could be longer-shorter-curlier-straighter. She's not a ten but, hey, a seven's not bad.*

In Sunday School I believe with every cell of my little-girl body that God and Jesus love me. We sing the song every week, *Jesus loves me this, I know. For the Bible tells me so.* But here's the deal, puberty floods me with doubt about God's love. Jesus is born, bloodlessly to a virgin mother while I began dripping blood monthly. Maybe Jesus no longer loves me?

I long, every Christmas Eve, to play the Virgin Mary in the Christmas play. I want to be her for at least one evening gazing lovingly at a plastic doll wrapped in a blanket. Church tells me God placed that baby in Mary's stomach because she is pure of heart, all virginal and good, the guiding standard for females. Was I still a good girl with hormones and blood pumping through me? I know I was never chosen to play the Virgin Mary.

Here's the worst thing: Estrogen drowns my rogue, chases moonlight from beneath my skin, and splinters me into a host of disparate pieces. Free-and-easy is stolen from my body, and Jesus-God shifts from loving to judging. Self-consciousness replaces self-assuredness and leaves me wandering, all alone.

◉

Two minutes, twenty seconds. Liquid-gold lyrics ooze elixir-like through my heart. The song of my soul. I play the record so often I feel I own it; Shelly Fabares, singing just for me, a name, just a name: Johnny Angel.

The record is all mine, bought with my babysitting money at Sages, our local department store, my first 45 RPM. I play that small disc, again and again, on my one-at-a-time record player.

Johnny Angel. When the song ends, I gently raise the arm of the record player and guide the needle back to the first groove. Reverentially. There is always a crackle when you hit that groove, an instant of static before Shelly sings again those two minutes and twenty seconds of lyrical love for Johnny Angel.

Johnny is my prayer, my plan for the future, my salvation. My young heart longs to be transported to heaven courtesy of Johnny.

My bleeding body feels dumped by Jesus, but Johnny arrives to take his place. Johnny, sweet Johnny, now shivers my skin.

A tug-of-war springs to life inside of me. Team Jesus or Team Johnny? Does Jesus still find me precious and good with breasts, blood, and pubic hair? Would he approve if I hook up with Johnny Angel? The Sunday school I had loved let me run and swing on the playground on Sunday mornings, taught me songs, gave me sweet red punch. Now church is hard pews and long lectures.

Jesus and Johnny Angel both promise heaven: one through God and the other through a boy's kiss. The promise of sweet kisses wins out. Boys are my obsession, my religion. Mark Brown, Bob Speidel, Dick Peterson. Crushed by my crushes, I desperately want one of those boys to notice me, flirt with me, love me with the same burning heart that Johnny Angel throbs inside my chest.

Privacy is hard to come by in our crowded house. Seven humans— Mom, Dad, my older brother, twin brothers three years younger than me, and my younger sister born three years after the twins—strain within the confines of 1,400 square feet with one bathroom. A stucco house built smack on top of the San Andreas Fault. The shaky earth echoes my own morphing body. Nothing is grounded or safe. I am Gumby. Pliant, twisted, curved, and reshaped as I stand by praying fervently that boys will like the final product.

Johnny is who I turn to when I snatch a quiet moment, alone in the bedroom I share with my younger sister. On my bed, eyes closed, the promise of Johnny Angel washes over me. I am in heaven, carried up and away from house and parents and noise and siblings and judging Jesus and my changing body and tender heart. For two minutes and twenty seconds, the music levitates me into free-floating space and time and everyone else shuts up.

◉

The girls' shower at Del Vallejo Junior High features pale-green tiles and labyrinthian paths with spewing showerheads. A sharp turn left lands you in an aisle of air-drying and another jag left into the drying room where you grab from a stack of scratchy white towels.

I adore gym class at Del Vallejo where we wear red shorts and a white blouse I take home once a week to wash. By the ninth grade, I am thrilled to be selected as a Junior Coach responsible for warming up the girls' classes with calisthenics before they head to one of many ball-centered sports: volleyball, handball, softball, or basketball.

"Go, You Chicken Fat, Go!" is my favorite. I lead daily a group of about twenty-five girls with the song blaring from a tinny speaker behind me: *Touch down every morning, ten times! Not just now and then. Give that chicken fat back to the chicken. Don't be chicken again. Go, you chicken fat, go!*

Another favorite song implores us to grow bigger boobs, which all of us flat-chested young girls take seriously. In this exercise, you stand tall, elbows bent at shoulder level and then move elbows toward each other behind your back then straighten both arms long to each side and move straight arms toward your back. Bend elbows again and repeat, all the time chanting together: *We must, we must, we must improve our bust. For fear, for fear, for fear we won't wear a brassiere.*

Toe touches, burpees, jumping jacks, and twists. My body loves them all. I was born to run, climb trees, sweat, and move. Naturally coordinated, I excel at most sports and would have been thrilled to lead gym classes all day long.

On the few rainy days at my Southern California junior high school, we cram all our pent-up energy into the fifteen-by-twenty-foot drying room. The small space transforms into our very own American Bandstand. We lug the tinny speaker inside and balance it on the green tile ledge that separates the showers from the rest of the gym. Instead of jumping jacks, we chase away chicken fat with all the latest dance moves.

Paramount among them: "Louie Louie." Dance in those days was not free-form wiggling but instead choreographed movements like the Mashed Potato, Watusi, the Stroll, and the Twist.

I have no interest in understanding the lyrics of "Louie Louie." The beat lures me in and gets my body moving. Dancing to "Louie Louie" requires us to form two lines facing each other on either side of the drying room. One of the lines shuffles to the left with two-beats while the other line shuffles right. And then reverse. Slide, slide back and forth while our arms move hula-like in sync with our legs.

Louie, Louie, oh, oh, Me gotta go,

Up until seventh grade, I had played catcher on a girls' softball team. I adored the game and could easily connect bat to ball and send it soaring into left field. I loved stealing bases, hollering, and tagging people out with the fat softball held firmly in my mitt. Now I moon and wait and wish and hope for boys to like me, which bores my rogue to death. I imagine that one night, worn out by my passivity and eagerness to conform, my sweet rogue leaps from my body and exits stage left.

I swear I hear her belt out loud and lusty: *Me Gotta Go.*

◉

My addiction to perfection blossoms when I am thirteen. Mom takes me to Kinney's Shoe Store to buy me Easter shoes, and I fall in love with a pair of red patent leather slip-ons with a red bow on each toe. But there's more: a matching red patent leather purse, a clutch with the same bow across its belly. Mom buys me the purse too. My Easter outfit is a black skirt with a white top trimmed with black piping. No little girl pink or lilac. I am black and white sophistication obsessed with perfecting my outfit.

The Little Store, our neighborhood five-and-dime, is a ten-minute bike ride from our house. A red bow for my hair. Small and clip on. I must have one. I count my babysitting money and know I have enough to cover the cost. I jump on my bike and pedal as fast as I can to the Little Store, which was officially named Stimson's. Mrs. Stimson takes my money and as I pay her I babble about my Easter outfit and shoes and purse. She puts my bow in a small bag, and I ride home.

I clip the bow into my hair and admire myself in the mirror. I notice my hand in the mirror and know I need a ruby ring. I must have a splash of red for my hands. I jump back on my bike and pedal even faster. I am possessed, driven by an inner fire with a single goal: perfection. I pedal furiously, my eyes focused on the road, to get there before they sell out of rings and I won't have enough red accents. I am out-of-my-body driven by dreams of how beautifully perfect I will look on Easter Sunday.

"Do you have rings?" I pant at Mrs. Stimson.

"We sure do, dear," and she motions me to a display of rings in all shapes and colors. All within my budget. I find a simple red stone with gold band, narrow, sleek. Mrs. Stimson bags it, and I'm on my way.

My addiction to perfection, born that Easter, flourishes in adulthood. I spend thousands of dollars on DKNY clothes and matching shoes, jewelry that dangles, and just the right shade of nylon. My pursuit of perfection holds me captive for years and keeps my rogue, disdainful, watching from a distance.

Dear Surfer Boys,

You are tan, muscled, and blond. You wear swimsuits called baggies and carry surfboards that weigh nearly thirty pounds. Southern California, 1960s. You reign from atop the evolutionary chart right up there with rulers and kings. I watch you swagger and strut, deeply comfortable in your boy bodies, on the cusp of men-bodies, your young skin slathered with suntan lotion that neon-glows you beneath the afternoon sun.

Do you know my best friend Susi and I watch your every move? She and I in our fourteen-year-old bodies, clad in two-piece bathing suits (you are too young for bikinis, our mothers tell us) hers navy blue with a skirt and mine pink-checked and covering my navel.

I know, sweet surfer boys, you never look at us, never crank your neck for a second glance. We are humble, know we are not worthy. We study the girls who walk beside you, bikini-clad, flat stomached, breasts, taut skin, bronzed and glowing. We know what we are not.

Brown-haired Susi and I, friends since kindergarten, squeeze lemon juice on our hair praying for streaks of blond while your surfer girlfriends parade and toss thick blond locks. Flirty flips, the crowning glory of these queens of Newport Beach.

Love me. Notice me. You are the ones, surfer boys and girls, who plant inferiority deep into my pubescent heart. I know I will never measure up but still I pray, wish, and hope. Please make me, someday, somehow, as beautiful, as comfortable and cocky in my skin, as all of you.

Mom never utters the word "sin" nor was it talked up in church. Southern California Methodists are not a sin-fearing lot. But I know, without a doubt, virginity is the law. Mom was born in 1920, and raised according to the strict rules of her Southern Methodist Church in Amarillo, Texas: "No alcohol. No dancing. No card playing. No sex before marriage."

Mom shed a few of these thou-shalt-nots when she married. She rarely drank but loved to dance her way through the kitchen shaking her right index finger and wiggling her hips as she sang, *I went truckin' on down the avenue without a single thing to do.* She also played a mean game of canasta and hearts. The blessed commandment of virginity, which was not on Moses's Top Ten tablet but might as well have been, was mandated for her daughters. No discussion. Sacrosanct.

My budding sexuality hones my talent for repression.

Dad is silent on the topic but Mom's fealty to virginity tattoos on my skin. *Wait until marriage, good girls don't, he will not respect you.* As passion bubbles and brews, I have no choice but to ignore my inner roiling. Throughout high school, I attend church every Sunday and am active in the Methodist Youth Fellowship (MYF). *Good girl* is stamped on my forehead, a label I wear proudly. As a rule follower and God believer, I will not let my mother or God down.

Repression works until Jim arrives my senior year of high school. My first steady boyfriend. We had gone to junior high together but in January of our senior year, romance sparks as we slow-dance to "Love Is Blue." Jim is a good boy, not a rule breaker either, and I his first steady girlfriend. My steadfast commitment to virginity teeters when Jim and I connect and I am confronted with a warm-blooded, breathing, tan, and lovely human being.

We become master kissers, sitting in Jim's blue Ford Fairlane in front of my house after dates, until we realize my little sister is spying on us from the bedroom window. We find a new spot a few blocks away at the edge of an empty lot across the street and kiss until our lips swell.

Jim asks me to go steady on May 11 at the senior prom. I say yes. We hold hands on graduation day. July 12, 1968, six months after we began dating, is a hot Friday night in San Bernardino, CA. *The Lion in Winter* with Peter O'Toole and Katherine Hepburn is playing at the Baseline Drive-In Theater, and we have a date.

Look God, I plead many times, *we are going steady. This is true love. Doesn't that make sex ok?* Several diary entries profess my deep love for Jim while other entries reveal my eagerness to break up. I am eighteen years old with my first serious boyfriend and have been dating him for six months. Love?

We pull into a slot far away from the screen and hook the metal box into the driver-side window. Jim buys popcorn and soda at the concession stand. A shimmering bottle of Coca-Cola dances on the large drive-in screen dancing to the lyrics, *Life is so much fun when you're refreshed.* I nibble a few bites of popcorn not wanting my mouth too salty or greasy.

"Want to get in the back seat?" Jim asks. "We could stretch our legs a bit and I could get out from behind this steering wheel."

"Yes," I say more quickly than I probably should have, my "good girl" status at risk. We settle in the back seat, popcorn-less, ice melting in our Cokes. The movie starts but we can't see with our eyes closed and lips locked together.

We sit on the passenger side of the back seat, our bodies twisted awkwardly toward one another. Steam clouds the side windows and inches its way toward the windshield. Our kisses blend from lips to open mouths to tongues probing and thrusting, pulling back and thrusting again.

"Are you comfortable?" Jim asks.

"I'm okay," I say, even though my torso twists awkwardly toward Jim while both knees remain pointed toward the front seat.

A few more minutes and our bodies align. I shift my legs up to seat-level and Jim does the same. Lying on our sides long across the back seat we mold face to face, belly to belly, thigh to thigh, our ankles braided together. The eagle has landed.

The passion I had kept contained seizes the opening. My guard is not only down, he has left the building. Jim's right hand eases atop my breast. I arch my back and offer up both breasts. The touch of his hand on my breast breaks me open. Desire envelops me, arches my back more deeply, pulls my blouse and bra up exposing my breasts. Flesh to flesh. The voices of my mother and God are silenced by the roar inside of me. My ears are shut tight. I hear nothing, consumed by passion-lust-desire, my every nerve-ending on high alert.

"We should slow down," Jim whispers and then repeats, louder.

"It's okay," I plead. I grab his hand and move it toward my crotch. He is now on top of me. I breathe in his warmth, feel the long heft of him. My hand finds his crotch, and I stroke his penis. Both of us still clothed from the waist down. He is hard. I am wet. I want this.

Jim sits up. Abruptly. I yank my hand away from his crotch, sit up, and pull my bra and blouse back in place. I take a few deep breaths, comb my hands through my hair. Shame courses through me.

"I'm sorry." I am nearly in tears. The voices of mother and God now booming in my head. Guilt and shame flood my body. My juice and passion skulk away, ducking into a hiding spot behind the jail cell of my ribs.

"It's okay," he says, his arms around me, comforting. "We both did it. I just think we would be sorry tomorrow."

Shame, sin's residue, floods my body. I tilt my head up toward the ceiling of the car, look to heaven, and pray silently to God. *I'm sorry, I'm sorry.*

◉

I want a DNA expert to slice into my bones, sample a drop of blood, or test the mucous I leave in a Kleenex. There must be evidence deep in my DNA that I carry knowledge of a time when female sexuality and passion were revered, respected, encouraged, and worshipped. It would help to know DNA of the ancient ones remains alive inside me.

Today's world demands proof. Real proof. No silly dream images that our culture blames on spicy food. So cut into me, goddamn it. Epigenetics does not lie. Slide a sample of me beneath your microscope. It will prove I danced in candlelit circles with other women draped in animal fur, skin oiled with rosemary, sweat dripping to earth. We danced in caves and temples dedicated to Hathor, Isis, Inanna, Ishtar. Holiest of the holy females led by priestesses dedicated to their honor.

I participated, my genes will prove, in the Eleusinian Mysteries of ancient Greece, the oldest of their kind that was celebrated each year for at least a thousand years, until 329 CE, during the reign of Emperor Constantine who, most assuredly, loathed and feared female mystery and sacredness.

The festival starts in early September in Eleusis, a town fourteen miles from Athens, and is considered the most mysterious of the ancient Greek world that gave life to the myth of Demeter and her daughter Persephone. The mysteries, while a tightly held secret, honor mother-daughter love and grieve daughter rape and kidnap into the gates of Hell. The quest, at its core, is spiritual enlightenment.

Here's what my dreams describe and my DNA will prove: Torches light a cave or goddess temple. We swig wine from a goat-belly water-skin and clasp animal bones between our teeth. We wear sacred beads that clack and clang as we dance. Our hands float above our heads as we sway our hips in rhythm to a sistrum, a musical instrument made of wood, bone, ivory, clay, and bronze. Throbbing and alive. Our every cell chocked full of sacred reverence. Sexy souls, the holiest of the holy.

We dance to honor the changes in female bodies. We dance when blood arrives and when it stops its monthly flow. We dance when passion, healthy and alive, rises in girls' bodies. We dance to honor sexuality that is nothing more or less that then wondrous expression of human life. We dance to honor birth and death.

My DNA confirms the truth of my imagination. My DNA proves that my memory of sacred rites was birthed by actual experience, traces of which root deep inside of me, golden threads woven through my cells right alongside my womb-time memories.

My body recalls the time of BCE, before the common era. Before BCE gave way, grudgingly, to CE, the common era, when humans fell in love with words, rationality, conquer, and control and fell out of love with female power, sacredness, intuition, and instinct.

DNA-transmitted shame lurks inside of me, and my *Lion in Winter* passion brings it to life. The more I repress and wallow in shame about passion, the more I push my sweet rogue far away. But rogue-energy hides in a place near my heart, sheltered by my ribs, hovering and waiting for me to awaken from my virgin-trance.

Shame keeps me clothed and upright on nights Jim and I park close to my home. I pretzel my body around the stick shift of Jim's Ford Fairlane, lean toward him from the waist up, my lower body safely twisted to the right. We kiss for hours and fondle while fully clothed. I never again cross the line. Virgin-freeze locks my body down. I behave, and never again have to beg for forgiveness from the white guy in the sky.

⊙

Jim is nineteen and I am twenty the summer we marry. Three months before our wedding, Mom and I sit together in the den. I am nervous, take a deep breath, and manage to get out what is heavy on my mind: "I am not sure we can wait to have sex until the wedding."

What I was thinking but did not say, "Mom, I'm so horny. What's so bad about having sex and not being married?"

Silence.

Mom sits on one side of the room in Dad's favorite chair. I am on the other side on the couch against a short wall that separates the den from our kitchen. She stares at me, a long pause before she speaks.

"We can move the wedding up. We could get you married by July."

My heart sinks. I desperately want her blessing, not a date change.

"There's too much to do. It's okay. We can wait."

Our wedding is planned for August 23, 1970, at Del Rosa Methodist Church. Two days before the ceremony, on a wicked hot afternoon, Jim and I do it, two horny kids on a lime green rug in front of a droning window air conditioner in the duplex we had rented from my aunt and uncle whose home was on the same lot.

No one can do the math, I think to myself, terrified our first stab at intercourse, which lasts maybe five minutes and produces nothing but guilt and mathematical calculations, might get me pregnant. I figure if people did count the months they would say, "Look at that, she got pregnant on her wedding night."

We are half-lucky. No pregnancy, but nothing close to an orgasm either, which I knew nothing about. Five minutes after we tumble down on the lime green rug, we get up, zip and button, dust off our bums, and drive to my parents' home where dear friends gift us a wooden rocking chair as a wedding gift.

Why didn't I listen to my body screaming at me? A week before the wedding I sprout two fat hemorrhoids. (I never had them before and have never had them since.) My body also lands me in bed for hours each morning with nausea from my newly acquired birth control pills.

The hemorrhoids holler: *Hey, asshole, maybe this getting married so young and still in college is not the best idea.* My belly heaves: *You cannot really stomach this marriage thing.* I do not listen. My body tries to inform me I am too young to get married but I ignore its messages. Karen Carpenter's "We've Only Just Begun" plays often on my favorite station, KMEN-129, promising happily ever after. "White lace and promises" lure me outside and away from my body that the world keeps telling me to tame and distrust.

◉

I cling to Dad's arm as we walk slowly down the aisle. I am dressed in white, flanked by six bridesmaids swathed in pink dotted Swiss holding daisy bouquets. Nearly a virgin. My mother, apparently clueless, beams at me with pride. That night, we're exhausted from the more than three hundred people who attend. (*You looked like Barbie and Ken*, my sister tells me later, which feels like the highest compliment.) We spend the night at the Holiday Inn just outside of San Bernardino near I-10. The next morning, we drive to Los Angeles International Airport for our honeymoon flight to Acapulco, Taxco, and Mexico City.

Our first hotel room. A bed. No stick shift between us. We do not tear off each other's clothes; we do not drown each other in passionate kisses. We kneel and pray. Knees and hands tightly clasped. Holiness floods my body. *I will be a good wife*, I silently promise myself. Sex is now legal but feels unnatural. Signatures on a marriage license do not chase repression away.

Two years later, Jim is among the last men drafted by the US Army the minute he graduates from college. He is assigned to the military's White House Communications Agency, and we move to Washington, DC, in 1973 right after my college graduation. I had lived my entire life in my parents' house or my aunt and uncle's duplex. The long distance from my family those first few months smothers me with homesickness, but my rogue sniffs an opening in those three thousand miles and begins to stir to life inside of me.

BREAKING OUT

Only the truth of who you are, if realized, will set you free.
—Eckhart Tolle

WHAT BEGAN as a game night in October, with Mai-Tais as fuel, morphs into strip poker (my idea), which escalates into partner-swapping (also my idea). *Bob & Carol & Ted & Alice,* the wife-swapping movie, had been popular a few years earlier, so why not try a Jim & Jackie & John & Carol? Four years into our marriage, I am twenty-four, my rogue cranked and raring to go after twelve years of confinement.

John and Carol, married two years longer than Jim and me, had lived next door to us in San Bernardino in the adjoining duplex owned by my aunt and uncle. They were from upstate New York and the four of us became fast friends. They moved to Washington, DC, a few months before we did and were the only people we knew when we landed there in 1973.

They help us find our apartment. John, branch manager of Hamilton Bank and Trust, hires me as a teller. The four of us watch football games together on Sundays and play doubles tennis. Until that night.

John and Carol will arrive at 7 p.m. A game night so no worries about making a whole dinner. I had found a recipe for Mai Tais. One bottle of dark and one of light rum sit on the kitchen counter.

"Want a taste?" I ask Jim, as I stir the concoction with a long wooden spoon. Jim opens a bag of potato chips and stirs together onion soup and sour cream for the dip.

"Sure," he says. "Join me?"

Jim and I rarely drink but that night, before John and Carol arrive, I pour us each a small glass.

"I feel that," I say as the rum burns its way down my throat and into my belly. "Yum!"

They are good, aren't they," Jim agrees. We stand at the kitchen counter and bolt them back. I sway just a bit and grab hold of the counter.

Jim reaches for two more glasses to take into the dining room with the dip. I sneak another big pour in my glass and swig it down. *That is good*, I say to myself as the warmth slithers belly-deep.

John and Carol arrive, and we serve drinks all around at the dining room table. We chat and catch up, sipping our Mai Tais and shoving a chip or two into the dip.

"You wanna play poker?" I ask.

Jim deals the cards. Game night is on. By now, the rum has set up shop in my body and brain. I'm not slurring but feel silly and light-headed. Fearless and, okay, reckless.

"How about strip poker?" I suggest about twenty-five minutes into our game. By now, we are all tipsy and the yeses are unanimous.

I draw the first losing poker hand and take off my shoes. As blouses and shirts, shorts and socks fall to the floor, the warmth in my belly is now lust. We talk movies, and I bring up the wife-swapping movie *Bob & Carol & Ted & Alice*.

"We have a Carol," I say. "All we need are three more of us."

By this time, rationality has drowned in rum. Six bleary eyes look back at me and none of them say no. Still wearing my bra and panties, I make my way to the master bedroom with John. Jim and Carol take the guest room.

John's breath of sweet rum, soft pink tongue licking inside my cheek, lips with a hint of chap draw me in. I release. Our bodies blend sweat and saliva and the river that lubricates my vagina floods between us, so new, *oh please, go deeper, thrust longer, oh god oh please oh thank you.*

How long did we stay in those bedrooms? No idea. But I can still feel the awkwardness when we emerge, gather our clothes, and say goodbye to John and Carol. Jim and I leave dishes for the next morning and cocoon in our bed after they leave. We promise each other we will never swap again, and we do not. I do not promise to never be with John again.

I want more.

Over the next four weeks, John and I find private places to couple: the back of his car, a school parking lot, and once in John and Carol's apartment. The idea of never sleeping with him again never occurs to me. Jim is my husband, Carol my friend, and John my boss. None of those labels stand a chance against hot sex.

Here's how it ends, the affair not my marriage, which hangs together, barely, for another few years. We are in the vault, John and me, Saturday just after the bank closes at noon. John locks the bank doors, and I am supposed to be settling my teller drawer. The steel-doored vault, cool, hidden, proves too hard to ignore.

Carol's knock that day on the locked outer doors of the bank is loud enough to be heard through the front door and partially closed vault. She'd come to pick up John and arrives earlier than expected. Her knock rouses us like a cold splash of water, so ill-timed, so close. Carol is unconcerned about my satisfaction; she wants her husband to open the door.

Her knocks keep going as I quickly unwind myself from John's arms, tug at my sweater, unsmear my lipstick. He wrenches up his zipper and smooths his hair. In all the jostling and hurrying, I bump my elbow hard on one of the safety deposit boxes inside the vault.

"Hurry," John whispers, loud, his blue eyes clouded with a fear that transforms him from a glorious blur of lips, saliva, tongue, and hands to terrified husband, illicit lover. I rub my elbow, finish smoothing my skirt, and walk quickly out of the vault to my teller window where I pretend to count one-dollar bills.

John runs to unlock the door and Carol bursts through, her nose spitting smoke and fire. Our days as duplex neighbors in San Bernardino seem long ago. I vaguely remember how kind and naive we were then, newlyweds, a good, steady couple. I never dreamed I had it in me to deceive my husband and betray a friend.

"What were you doing?" Carol demands.

"Settling the drawers," John answers.

I stand behind the bars of my teller window, counting those ones and feeling ever so grateful for the fives, tens, and twenties. The bills smudge my fingers a dirty brown with their acrid, sweaty smell of the hundreds of hands they had passed through to pay for ice cream cones, prostitutes, bottles of beer, and wands of mascara before landing in my teller drawer.

Carol walks toward my window, and I struggle to reshape my face into some hint of innocence.

"Hey, Carol, I am nearly done here," I say while praying silently the smell of money trumps the smell of sex wafting off my body.

"I'm almost finished," I say again, trying to shrink beneath Carol's silent glare, my own eyes focused on the green of the bills. While I count, John straightens papers on his desk in the middle of the small branch office of Hamilton Bank and Trust. Carol plants herself at the mid-point between my teller window and John's desk, waiting for us to lock the vault door and walk out together into the October afternoon.

◉

The satiny fabric of our floral couch rubs at my bare bottom. My middle finger is pulled moth-like, again and again, to the eight thousand clustered nerve endings between my legs. I lean against throw pillows, mouth agape, face flushed. Breath. I am all breath: sharp intakes that draw heart-deep, slow at first and then building momentum, a melodic symphony inside of me with my cells playing strings, blood on percussion and bones on bass.

I am nearly twenty-five, and four years into our crumbling marriage. John and Carol have moved away and Jim and I are trying to patch our marriage back together. But another problem arises. I have discovered my clitoris and it is intent on busting me free.

In our apartment in Alexandria, VA, a suburb of Washington, DC, I am alone for the first time in my life when Jim travels on business. I buy my first tampons, which had been forbidden by my mom because they might break my hymen and steal my virginity. The tampons come with instructions to place a mirror in front of my vagina before I insert.

What was that nub?

My clitoral discovery fuels me with agency I had not felt since my years in the elm tree. The siren song of my rogue. A magic button that springs every ounce of me to life. I alone can turn my passion on and off and each time I do, curiosity, courage, wonder, and pleasure flood my body. I have no idea how to reconcile passion with my still thriving good-girl persona. I do know lust is here to stay and has planted me directly on top of the virgin-whore line that has been enshrined by the sands of time and culture. A line formed of barbed wire, pain-inflicting and treacherous. A line I am forced to walk on tiptoes, heels teetering off the ground. Unrooted, insecure, beautiful, and horny, walking the treacherous line that shifts and curves.

Dear Clit,

We need to talk. You wreak havoc when you spring to life between my legs. I am a good girl, believe in God, obey my parents, and am a dutiful wife. Except for my affair with John. And then you, literally, pop up. An electric zapper between my legs that steamrolls repression with unabashed joy.

Do you have a clue how good I was? I never ditched school, drank alcohol, smoked dope, or stayed out beyond curfew. I got home early so many times I never had a curfew. I got one poor work slip in eighth grade algebra for asking Mr. Haffner why algebraic equations made sense. I never shoplifted, talked back to a teacher, or threw a party when my parents were out of town. I was on the Honor Roll and Student Council. When my girlfriends at Judy Johnson's slumber party snuck out of her house to toilet paper Bob Speidel's house, I said no. Not right. I was the only one who stayed behind.

My brother Danny, two-and-a-half years older, is the bad boy hell-raiser of our family. He excels as a bad boy which leaves only the mantle of good-girl achiever for me as second child, oldest daughter.

Danny is not a juvenile delinquent by any means but he tests my parents. He is a football player big and strong, and whets my ambition-gene by wiping me out, with reckless abandon, in every game of Risk and Monopoly that Mom makes him let me play. My own "I'll-show-you" grit is a byproduct of those brutal games. Danny smokes dope, stays out late, and has regular sex with his high school girlfriend. My parents need a break, and I am up to the task. Here's the truth: I wear the cloak of Good Girl with pride and a deep longing for the world to notice just how damned good I am.

As a devoted wife when we are too poor to afford a vacuum cleaner, I hang our lime green area rug, room-size, over the clothesline and smack it with a broom. Jim and I are counselors for the junior high church group. I sing in the church choir. We pay all our bills on time and are full-time college students while working four part-time jobs between us. I balance our checkbook religiously each month.

My goodness keeps me afloat for twenty-four years, waning only when we move three thousand miles away from all the people and institutions I strive to please. Geography opens my eyes, and you, sweet clit, seal the deal. Come on down, you coax and cajole. My fingers obey, and each zap of divine pleasure issues a single vibrating command: Know Yourself.

Jim and I, our marriage crumbling beneath us, take a weekend away in Virginia Beach in Southern Virginia. We were both born and raised an hour from the Pacific Ocean with its biting cold water in June, big waves, wide stretches of sand, palm trees, brilliant sunsets, and dry air courtesy of the nearby desert. We lived close enough to the Pacific Ocean that sea gulls circled through our valley on wind drifts blowing off the ocean.

We arrive after dark on a Friday night in Virginia Beach, a four-hour drive from our apartment in Alexandria, Virginia. We find a parking place near the ocean's edge, take off our shoes, and dig our toes into the cool sand.

Our conversation on the drive down rambles from work stuff, to a trip to Hawaii my younger sister was taking with her school choir, to the RV my father has just purchased. This trip is not for heavy talk. We have come to see if our marriage has hope.

My heart races at my first glimpse of the Atlantic but it is pitch-black and low tide. Jim and I walk to the water's edge and see white-tips of foam on waves that seem lethargic, barely able to lap their way to our toes at the water's edge.

It's more lethargic than the Pacific Ocean, I think as I peer through the dark, my hand holding Jim's but not feeling the currents of our early years. The next morning, we walk from our motel back to the beach following a row of pine trees that line the way. Pine trees. So wrong. Beaches do not have pine trees. I long for palm trees, the soft rush of fronds in a late afternoon breeze. Instead, the sharp bite of pine sap smells out of sync with the salty ocean air. Oil to the ocean's water. Wrong.

The air also disappoints. Instead of the arid blue of the Pacific Ocean, this sky feels like a thick blanket, heavy-humid-gray, weighted. I had never experienced humidity at the beach. Everything feels awkward, wrong, just as my hand does when I slip it into Jim's.

High tide greets us that morning but still the waves seem smaller, the ocean older, more tired, the thick humid air dulls the water's sun-sparkle. My heart sinks. Our beach trip is intended to jumpstart our nearly dead marriage, a reboot for Jim and me by the ocean spirits that grew us.

"What do you think?" I ask Jim. It was also his first glimpse of the Atlantic.

"It's different," he agrees. "Not as sparkly." I squeeze his hand and squeeze back the tears that threaten to spill down my cheeks. I know, heart-deep, I cannot stay in my marriage. I know I had come on this trip so it would look like I wanted to save us, but I am play-acting. My guilt over hurting Jim is enormous, but my need to get to know who I am as a sexual adult female burns larger. No prayers can save us.

CONFUSION

I'm embarrassed. I'm not a real person yet.

—Greta Gerwig, *Frances Ha*

WHEN I HIT PUBERTY, Mom gives me a booklet I still own today entitled *You're a Young Lady Now.* The cover art features a young girl dressed in what were then called dungarees, a white blouse, hair in pigtails. She sits at a vanity with a ruffled white skirt and stares into the mirror. Staring back at her is a sleeker version of herself with hair neat and curled, a lilac bow clipped on each side of her face, a lilac dress, and pearls. The "who" she will be as a young lady looks back at her.

I stare at the lilac-bedecked girl and wonder if I will ever be that pretty.

"Do I get to keep this?" I ask Mom.

"Yep. It's all yours." My insides quiver as the booklet passes from her hands to mine.

"Read through and let me know if you have any questions."

A few weeks earlier, we are shown at school a sex education film. Boys in one room and girls in another. I glance through the booklet and see diagrams similar to what I had seen in the film: fallopian tubes and dotted lines showing how eggs wiggle over and then drop down. I have no idea inside of me where all the stuff is, but I do know from the way adults act when they talk about this stuff that it's big.

Mom picks up the elastic belt.

"You slip this under your panties," she explains, showing me how to loop the end tabs of the napkin through the belted hooks. The idea I might try a tampon is not within the realm of possibility since Mom is convinced that stuffing a wad of cotton into my vagina will break my hymen and strip me of my virginity.

I watch her demonstration closely, memorizing the direction and loop of the two flaps on the end of the pad.

"You have to change your pads regularly," she tells me. "The most blood will come the first few days but then it eases up."

I don't have many questions and am eager to gather my treasures and go to my bedroom. Once there I study the booklet which tells me to "keep sweet and clean at all times." Get "plenty of sleep so you'll be good humored and full of pep." The word "blood" makes an appearance only once as a monthly "flow of watery fluids and a small amount of blood." The booklet prefers "a little red stain" to the actual use of the word "blood." A dainty little red stain, so ladylike, no need to fuss.

The booklet makes no mention of my clitoris or lust. In truth, I am as ignorant about my body at twenty-five as I was at twelve. In 1973, *Our Bodies, Ourselves* has just been published. Plastic specula are available to insert in your vagina to see the inner ridges and curves. Sex is seeping out of dark corners and into the light.

Walking away from my marriage means I am alone with the virgin-whore, good-girl/bad-girl conundrum that plays me like a drum from the inside out. I know lust is here to stay but have little idea how to integrate it, healthy and whole, into my body, my life. I am alone in Washington, DC, a big city full of lusting young lawyers in a body that has blossomed into beauty. Three thousand miles from family and lifelong friends and furiously intent on appearing smart and in control.

What can go wrong?

I fall in love first with Princeton, a lawyer at the Civil Aeronautics Board (CAB) in Washington, DC. Hard and fast, my heart unbothered by the fact I am still legally married to Jim. I am a new reporter for the *Aviation Daily,* a yellow-papered newsletter that reports on the aviation industry. CAB, the airline regulatory agency, fills six floors of an office building on Connecticut Avenue.

My young and beautiful façade papers over an inner tangle of insecurity, anxiety, and horniness. The dating world is brand new, and I am figuring it out in a building packed with horny lawyers from Ivy League colleges. I have landed in a tank of piranhas circling young, pretty me for the kill.

My California roots stand me out as a sun-kissed shiksa in this east coast city. Princeton takes note. He is Catholic not Jewish but is intrigued by my California-ness. He had just broken up with a long-term girlfriend; I am separated but legally married. Our timing sucks.

My orphan heart aches from the three thousand miles between me and my own family, and I fall hard and fast. Leaving Jim and breaking up our marriage had been my idea but still I ping-pong between exhilaration over my new freedom and the deep ache of loneliness.

Princeton invites me to his family's oceanfront beach home in Bethany Beach, Delaware, to celebrate the bicentennial, July 4, 1976. His entire family is there, and I fall in love with all of them. His younger sister wants to know everything about Beach Boy culture. His parents are refined and beautifully clothed in casual shades of lime green. Patriotism and celebration are on high boil that holiday weekend but Princeton never misses church. The Fourth is on Sunday so we attend mass at the local Catholic church at 5 p.m. Saturday. I press against him on the hard pew, loving the heat of his body while doing my best to ooze piety and purity.

A few weeks later, before we have the chance to consummate what feels to me like our deep love, he tells me it won't work. *You are still legally married,* he tells my breaking heart, *but we are separated,* I beg, *no chance of us getting back together,* I plead. *It feels morally wrong,* he counters with altar-boy sincerity and intent. I cannot fight his Catholic roots.

A smattering of Harvard grads come and go, one Dartmouth, a Columbia, and a Penn who would become one of my dearest friends. Here's the deal. The beauty that lights my face in my mid-twenties, much brighter than in high school, feels as if it suctions intelligence from my brain in big dollops. In high school, I was smart; now I am pretty. I figure it is hoggish to be both.

I land in Washington, DC, with a bachelor's degree in English from California State University, San Bernardino. Not exactly stellar credentials in our nation's capital, which someone once described as rife with overachieving student council presidents and valedictorians from all over the nation. When people ask where I am from, I never say San Bernardino but instead answer "near Los Angeles."

My insecurity hits its highest point and deepest pit when I meet Andy, a journalist visiting from New York. Ivy League? I have no idea but he is funny and opinionated with wavy dark hair. Andy invites me to visit him in New York City for a long weekend a few months after we meet, and I say yes. Jim actually drives me to Union Station for the train to New York. He fervently believes I will work wanderlust out of my system. I feel slimy for accepting his offer to drive me but grateful for the ride. Confusion runs rampant.

Andy picks me up at the train station in New York and takes me directly to his apartment where we tumble into bed. I do not recall if the sex was good or bad but that evening, we meet a group of his friends at a small, very New York, Italian restaurant. Three steps down, red-checkered tablecloths, the air thick with garlic. All of them are New Yorkers, writers and reporters, dark-haired, articulate, confident in their opinions, loud with their laughter.

Insecurity swallows me whole. I sit at that rectangular wooden table with conversation flowing around me and literally cannot speak. I am mute. Fully and totally mute. I smile stupidly, nod on occasion and feel dreadfully uncomfortable, but I cannot physically force words out of my mouth. The evening is interminable. The others try at first to engage me but then avoid my eyes. Talk around, over, and through me. I am the elephant in the room. I recognize now I was in the throes of a panic attack but at the time felt like a dead sea lion I once saw marooned on the beach, a lump waiting for the waves to wash me back to sea.

"What is wrong with you?" Andy spits at me as soon as dinner is over, and we are on the sidewalk walking back to his apartment. "You just sat there like an idiot." (I think he called me an idiot but it could have been my word because I felt myself a Class One Idiot.)

"I don't know," I answer honestly. We do not hold hands or touch as we walk the stained and smelly New York sidewalk back to his apartment. I have no idea how to explain myself. Like my hemorrhoids, it had never happened to me before and never happens again. I long to be back in San Bernardino with people who know and love me. Anywhere but this big cement city.

San Bernardino is only sixty miles west of Los Angeles, but I can count on one hand the number of times my family or Jim and I ventured into LA to see a play or visit an art museum. I was a small-town girl through and through. New York is chock-full of dark-haired, fast-talking, speed-walking, get-out-of-my-way-I'm-important-and-in-a-hurry people. Not a surfer boy or girl among them. I have landed on

Mars. What I do know, bone-deep, is that everyone is smarter than me, better than me. Inferiority rages beneath my pretty-girl face.

That night, I sleep in Andy's bed, and he takes the couch. The next morning, my train not leaving until 2 p.m., I am no longer mute but feel awkward as hell. We ride bicycles through Central Park and the bike he loans me has loud squawking brakes. He rides in front of me but turns and glares in my direction every time I hit the brakes that screech metal-on-metal.

It's your damn bike, I say to myself, *why didn't you get it fixed*. Of course, I do not voice these words, but I do hit the brakes a few extra times hoping the screech and squawk irritate him even more.

◉

The divorce papers from Jim's lawyer arrive in the mail one month after Mom's death in 1978. Jim has moved back to San Bernardino. I stay in Washington. He files the papers not knowing Mom is so close to dying.

Guilt lured me back to San Bernardino the previous summer to give my marriage one last try. That lasts about three weeks before I move back in with my parents and spend the summer driving up and down the coast of California looking for work. I am there when Mom has what we think is a stroke in late June 1977 that leaves her paralyzed on one side. By August, she is learning again to walk just as I land a job in Washington, DC, on a housing newsletter. I am moving back to Washington. Alone.

The night before I fly back east, Mom and I sit on the couch in the den.

"I shouldn't leave you," I say, near tears. "I tried to find a job out here. You know I did." I had interviewed in San Diego, San Francisco, and San Jose. Nothing.

"I know sweetie. You need to do this. You must follow your heart."

I take in her words. Try to let them ease my heart which is also struggling with torrents of guilt over leaving Jim.

"I really tried to make it work with Jim. I did try," I say to Mom. I take a deep breath. Pause for a long moment. "I'm so confused, Mom. I wish Jim were mean or something. I know I can't really explain it, but the marriage just doesn't work for me." Both my parents adore Jim, and I am the first of our family to divorce.

I lean my head on Mom's still strong left shoulder. Tears fall. I try to absorb every ounce of her warmth. As a Methodist, I had never been to confession in my life but feel an overwhelming need for Mom's blessing. Bless me though I am nearly divorced. Bless me though I am moving back east and leaving you here crippled. Bless me because I am a screwed-up horny mess and don't know what I am doing.

"Make a good life for yourself," she offers. It will be last time I see her fully conscious. Alive.

We celebrate Mom's miraculous recovery on New Year's Eve 1977. I am on the east coast and can't afford the trip home, but in January, Mom and Dad plan a trip to visit me in my brand-new apartment in Arlington, Virginia. Dad calls just as I slide a tray of homemade chocolate chip cookies, made especially for them, into the oven.

"Mom's sick again," he tells me. "We can't make the trip."

I sink into the couch, hugging the phone between my shoulder and chin.

"How bad is it?"

"It's bad, sweetheart. They are running tests but think it's brain cancer."

Brain cancer. My breath catches in my throat, sticks there, not wanting to find its way out into a world that will too soon not include my mother.

Three months later, Mom dies. She had lain in white silence for eleven days with bandages swathed elegantly around her head like a turban. They cut her open in search of cancer, and I imagine the jagged scar beneath the bandages, slashing diagonally across the shaved half of her dark hair, angry and raw from the futile surgery that steals her voice and consciousness. I arrive in San Bernardino after Mom is in surgery.

Too much cancer. Opened her up, closed her up, the surgeon tells us in a barrage of words, few of which I hear. I focus, instead, on images of things you open and close: jewelry boxes, safe deposit boxes, trash cans. Too much cancer, nothing we can do, closed her up, left her at the curb.

Eleven days of silence, coma, waiting. The antiseptic hospital smell permeates the air like stale perfume.

Wake up, I plead silently for too many hours of those eleven days, praying fervently to Sky God, Mother God, and any other God who might listen. I long for a last word, a tidbit of wisdom, a guiding hand. Mom's freckled hands lay silent by her side, the flesh tone a reprieve from the smothering white of bandages, sheets, walls. Flesh of my flesh, blood of my blood.

I want to touch, stroke, kiss, and hold her hands. No. I want more. Her hands are my focus, my obsession; I want to lick, suck, suckle, latch on.

I'm not done yet, I pray to her silent form. *Give me, give me, give me.*

A fact: Mammals typically lick their offspring clean immediately after birth to free the newborn from the amniotic sac, to clean and dry the baby's fur, and to stimulate breathing and digestive processes in the newborn.

I long to lick her back to life. Or, maybe she can tuck me into some unseen amniotic sac inside her dying womb and rebirth me to the other side with her. Life without her is unimaginable.

Mom dies on Palm Sunday, March 19, 1978. I am a still-under-construction-twenty-eight-year-old, my heart broken by her rapid death. They autopsy her and find tiny cells of cancer littering her kidneys, lungs, brain. My grandmother yells at my father across her dead daughter's body: "You will not cut my baby open," but she loses the battle. Dad needs to know what stole his wife.

I still have the yellowing autopsy report in a special file labeled "Mother." It tells me the weight of her spleen and heart and notes the beginnings of Crohn's disease in her fifty-eight-year-old body. (*My mother the crone*, I think to myself when I first read the report.) I also have a single lock of her still-black hair I keep in a blue envelope in a locked metal box. Every few years, I hold the hair carefully between my thumb and index finger, rub the soft strands against my cheek, longing for the ghost of a scent which has long been extinguished.

Dear Wine Bottles,

Uncork me, you whisper, when I open the refrigerator to grab some spinach, an apple. Drink me, you lure through long sensuous fingers of fragrance that caress my jaw, my cheeks. Pour me, you insist, into fat rounded glasses.

Amber, Burgundy, white, pale pink. You arrive in colors to match every mood, gifting me liquid fire. You stir my rogue to life inside me but it is a false impression. Rogue is rooted and knows where she needs to go, while wine fuels me with fake courage, becomes my partner in seduction. Ego-juice that empowers me at night but leaves me lonely in the morning. I do not sink into alcoholism but welcome liquid courage on nights I feel insecure.

One glass releases me into the moment, chases away yesterday and tomorrow worries with liquid mindfulness. Take, drink. They do not call liquor "spirits" for nothing. Your blessings permeate my body, mute my guilt, and enflame my passion.

Remember that night I sat in that five-star restaurant with my handsome date, only him across from me, so sleek and elegant? My nails, long and blood red, and my right index finger, so light, so dexterous, circles the rim of the wine glass, again and again. My dating skills are much improved. I nestle the glass close to my heart, between my breasts, and lean toward him, elbows on the table, eyes on him, just him.

I flash a Mona Lisa smile, my green eyes boring through him, drawing him into my web of mystery and desire until he tumbles. Ensnared.

He sits spellbound by my beauty, the soft lure of me and the fine linen tablecloth and two tapered candles, slow-pulsing flames, all the other diners hushed and distant. My silk blouse, a subtle shade of ivory, caresses the beauty of my breasts, offers a hint of cleavage, a dash of modesty as my heart beats slow and patient beneath the folds of silk.

You, sweet wine, imbue me with the power-over sensation of seduction. One more slow turn around the rim and he is mine. He motions for the check, two fingers signaling, as I sip my last swallow of wine and slip my manicured hand into his. We walk out together. Holy lust, hallowed desire in my every stardust cell.

Guilt pulses through me like bulbous black thunder clouds. Loud and threatening. Shame's nasty sidekick. My dead mother and abandoned husband deliver a one-two punch that splits me asunder, allowing grief and shame to slither through my every pore.

Guilt over my dead mother? I moved far away from her when she was still crippled and just relearning how to walk. Three thousand miles. Could I have saved her if I stayed in California?

Shame over divorcing my husband? Why couldn't I have remained a dutiful wife and had babies with Jim? We never had children. I wonder if guilt and shame scared me away from even trying to get pregnant? Too much death and divorce early in my life left me fearful of the vulnerability of motherhood.

I stay busy and try to keep guilt and shame at bay. But in the darkness of night, they crank through my brain on hamster wheels of "why" and "if only." My anguish locks me in the past, reexamining my choices, but also dampens my dreams of the future.

Why can't I release you? If only I could.

NEW PATHS

Now we are going to make a new path . . . And you dig in all directions: up and down, in and out, right and left. Nothing natural or interesting goes in a straight line.
—Sherry Ruth Anderson, *The Feminine Face of God*

HER DARK HAIR is gray-streaked and hangs down her back. Small-boned, petite, a former nun and now Jungian analyst, Anne Lewandoski lives on the sixth floor of an apartment complex on Connecticut Avenue in Washington, DC. Her small rectangular apartment has narrow windows and a west-facing sliding-glass door heavily shaded by towering oak trees. Her home feels womb-like to me, cloistering not claustrophobic; her presence is calm and welcoming. Death and divorce double-teamed me, broke my heart. I need help.

A former boyfriend recommends Anne. "She's a Jungian," Joe tells me. "You will focus a lot on your dreams." I know little about the Swiss Analyst Carl Jung, but I do know I need help.

In our first session, Anne describes her Jungian approach and says, "I will need you to keep a dream journal. Will you be able to do that?"

I stare into her brown eyes, the same color as my mother's, and am flooded by memories of snuggling with Mom on the couch as a young girl sharing my dreams.

"Yes," I whisper, fighting back tears.

She leans toward me, places her hand on top of mine. "Are you ok?"

"Mom and I shared dreams when I was little. It's been a long time."

"You've come to the right place," Anne says as she pats my hand and sits back in her chair. "Bring your journal each week," she explains. "We will focus on the dreams you write down. Watch for symbols and metaphor. Every detail is a message."

My dreams, as if aware of my renewed attention to their every detail and respect for their wise counsel, do not disappoint. Mother dreams tumble out of me. In one, Mom is a cadaver I long to breathe back to life. In another, she bakes me cookies, honey-rich and golden. I break one cookie open and marvel at the long golden DNA-like strands of honey. In another she is in the bathroom, door shut. I stand on the other side and the smell of her shit wafts through me like an elixir. I realize how much I long for her smell. The fully human shit, stink, and wonder of her.

◉

Sweet Nike, the ancient Greek goddess of victory, inspires me to claim the power of my feet pounding on asphalt and the strength of sweat. She pumps my blood and sets the tongues of my heart singing. Anne helps me to unbreak my heart but my body needs reclaiming too. A pair of Nike running shoes to the rescue.

The first day I lace up my brand-new Nikes is a Sunday morning. Dressed in new running shorts and top, I announce to my roommate I am going running.

She looks up from the *New York Times*, her eyes dubious but smile encouraging. "Good for you!"

I live in Colonial Village, not far from Key Bridge that spans the Potomac River from Rosslyn, Virginia, to Georgetown. It's a five-mile run to Georgetown, there and back, that I will cover many times as I build speed and endurance, but that day, that Sunday morning, my all gets me a single block up Key Boulevard to Veitch Street and back. An uphill climb at least that totals maybe one-tenth of a mile. When I return to our apartment my roommate is still reading, most likely the same *New York Times* article. She looks up, does not roll her eyes but says, "That was quick."

She is right, but that brief sprint sparks my love affair with running, which proves to be as enduring as my love affair with dreams. Running whispers sweet-somethings in my ear, convinces me I am strong, in my own body, just me. Sweat replaces guilt with gratefulness, and I wear half-moon sweat stains as medals of pride. My dreams journey me beyond linear time while running roots me body-deep, fully present.

I run my first 10K race, sponsored by Bonne Bell in 1980, one year after I begin therapy with Anne. Running does for my body what Anne does for my ego and soul: lands me home. I have a picture of me beaming as I cross the Bonne Bell finish line in sky-blue running shorts. Over the years I have completed the Marine Corps Marathon, two half-marathons, 20 milers, 15 milers, 10 milers, and too many 10Ks to count. I have run country roads and city streets of Maine, West Virginia, California, Arizona, New Mexico, New York, New Hampshire, Massachusetts, Vermont, Delaware, Virginia, Maryland, Pennsylvania, Florida, and Texas. I circled the US Capitol and monuments of Washington, DC, hundreds of times.

Each time I lace up my Nikes, I imagine the goddess Nike whispering in my ear: *Go. Feel healthy and whole in your body and soul. You've got this!*

⊙

What's the sin in this?

The question comes in a dream less than a year after my mother's death where a Jewish woman in her early twenties, dressed in contemporary clothes with chin-length black hair and brown eyes, interviews me for a class she is taking. She holds an ancient pot in front of my face.

"What's the sin in this?" she blurts out. I have no idea what she is talking about and think her tone is rude. She asks me what I think of her interview skills, and I tell her she is abrasive and should work on developing rapport.

She softens and then holds the gray ceramic pot closer to my face and asks again, "What's the sin in this?"

"Oh," I reply. "That's what you meant by your question."

The pot is rounded earthenware about eight inches wide and six inches high etched with hieroglyphics and animal figurines in raised relief including a cow and pig. I run my fingers across a rough spot I think are hieroglyphics.

"Ah, you're getting close," the woman says to me.

Just to the side of the rough spot, also in raised relief, is an old-fashioned wood-burning stove with a woman's arm protruding out of it. I realize that was the sin.

When I awaken, I write the details in my dream journal not mildly certain I have the answer. The hieroglyphics are indecipherable and the woman's arm extending out the oven door could represent many things: the horrific sin of the Holocaust? The women throughout history who have surrendered their frustrated creativity and lives to the heated gas of an oven? What about the hundreds of thousands of women burned at the stake because they trusted and acted on their own healing intuition and instinct for which they were branded witches and heretics?

The cow and pig? How many times have women been dismissed and silenced with words like, "She's a cow," and, "What a fat pig?" Or could the sin be that we eat animals?

Nothing rings true.

My dream screams *pay attention, figure it out.* I have no idea when I awaken what the answer is nor do I realize that the question will propel my search for self and soul. *What's the sin in this?* The question launches me on what will be a forty-year search for the answer. It takes me years to realize the woman's arm extending from the oven is trying to get my attention just like the female eyes in the Uffizi. *Go rogue. Be all that we could never be.*

◉

I meet Peter when I am thirty-two. A fine man, and a writer and producer with NBC radio and television in New York City who recently transferred to Washington, DC. By this time, I am working as a newspaper lobbyist for the American Newspaper Publishers Association. A good job but my soul is restless, always in search of more meaning, and my progress in therapy with Anne inspires me to ponder a career change. I want to be a psychotherapist.

On the night I meet Peter, our eyes lock across a room at the National Press Club one week before Christmas at a holiday party for my coed softball team. Peter is there with my teammate Steve, and I know as our eyes connect that I will beg Steve for an introduction.

But mine is not the story of a rescuing prince. A few months after I begin dating Peter, my dreams gift me with a true savior: the power of *shibboleth.* An ancient password of change and resurrection.

In the dream, I stand amid a large crowd of Romans all robed and togaed listening to a man on a raised stage, also in Roman garb, who keeps saying the word *shibboleth*. Everyone in that crowd thinks he is saying it wrong. I know he is pronouncing it correctly.

The minute I awaken I write down the dream in my purple journal and look up *shibboleth* in the dictionary. I had heard the word but had no idea what it meant. The dictionary offers a definition: *a custom that differentiates a class of people.* The definition also includes a Biblical reference, Judges 12:6, which I look up immediately. *Shibboleth* was used in ancient times as a password to separate out believers from nonbelievers. An ancient word of passage I knew the man had said correctly. My time for passage is now.

My daytime hours are full of fretting: Can I get over my terror and fall in love again with Peter? How can I pay for graduate school that I need for a new career as a therapist? Am I stupid to leave a decent paying job as a newspaper lobbyist because it doesn't feed my soul? Should I? Shouldn't I?

Shibboleth to the rescue. According to the Book of Judges, the word was used by the Gileadites to weed out believers from nonbelievers. Gileadites were believers in Yahweh who could pronounce the "sh" sound, but the nonbelieving Ephraimites dropped the "h" and pronounced it as "sibboleth", which got them killed. At least forty-two thousand Ephraimites pressed tongue tips to their top palate and were killed for being unable to pronounce the "sh" sound. I gotta say all the murdering in the name of God is disturbing, but, all that aside, the dream stirs me to action.

The Roman man on stage pronounces shibboleth correctly, and can pass into the promise land. It was my dream so I take it as my sign that I am ready to pass into new lands, give graduate school, and love, a shot. That very morning, I shift into gear, give notice at work and begin researching graduate degrees. I do not move in with

Peter right away but the dream reassures me that my heart, ripped to shreds by death and divorce, is ready to try again.

My shibboleth dream springs from the deepest interiors of my body and soul. Ancestral wisdom, straight out of Jung's collective unconscious, no outside experts required. The Uffizi eyes will come years later but spring from the same source. My deepest source of knowing.

Shibboleth does not land me in happily ever after—a state that does not exist. I do fall in love with research in graduate school and with my work as a therapist. I fall in love with Peter who is not a prince but a flesh-and-blood man who comes into my life at a point when my belief in myself has begun to take hold. I am ready to entrust my heart to another human being and my skills and talents to a new field of endeavor. I am stretching and learning, falling and getting up. I am fully human. My body sends neither hemorrhoid nor nausea as warning flares. The time is ripe for change.

◉

I am at Omega for a week in June 1993 to journey with Inanna, the widely revered Sumerian goddess of love, sensuality, fertility, and war. She is all that. A loud and lusty female revered in Mesopotamia thousands of years earlier who takes lovers and revels in her vulva outdoors beneath a huluppu tree. She lives large: ruthless and gentle, vindictive and kind, loving and murderous. I know with certainty, if you slice and dice my DNA, Inanna is in there large-as-life.

The workshop, Journey to the Temple of Inanna, is led by four actresses: Olympia Dukakis, Joan Macintosh, Lesley Avaysian, and Remi Bousseau, a troupe known as Voices from the Earth. We meet each morning in an octagonal wooden structure deep in the woods of Omega Institute in Rhinebeck, New York. Screens on all sides open to a lush green landscape with no apparent barrier between inside and out. Summer has parked itself on the land and languishes, full-blown, insect-biting.

I have a huge girl crush on Inanna, a mythic wonder woman who lived ferociously. A powerful goddess with an even more powerful sexuality. I had studied translations of her story including that of Samuel Noah Kramer, who wrote that Inanna was Sumer's "most beloved and revered deity . . . (who) played a greater role in myth, epic and hymn than any other deity, male or female." Male or female. My brain had absorbed the facts about Inanna, but I am eager to explore and feel her power through my body. I need to feel her dance through me and empower my voice. I am eager to spend a week learning body-deep, Inanna's female power and passion.

The timing is perfect. Ten years after my shibboleth dream led me to marry Peter and to complete graduate school, life throws another major change in my path. My father is diagnosed with lung cancer in May and refuses treatment. Mom's death fifteen years earlier had caught me by surprise, and I am not going to let that happen again. My plan is to be there for Dad through all stages of his dying.

By this time in 1993, I am director of the Washington, DC, office of Times Mirror, which is based in Los Angeles, only sixty miles west of Dad, who still lives in the house where I grew up. I had completed graduate school and worked for several years as a therapist while consulting for Times Mirror, but when the offer to lead the DC office as chief lobbyist comes through, I jump. With Dad only sixty miles from the office, I am able to see him often over his last months. I know I need Inanna energy to prepare for Dad's imminent death.

Olympia Dukakis explains on the first day that we will explore the many dimensions of the goddess and her dark sister Ereshkigal through our bodies, using movement and sound. No words.

"This is not therapy," she instructs the forty of us, all women aged nineteen to sixty.

"Don't try to analyze at all," Olympia warns. "Let sounds and movement flow through you. Your body is your instrument. Let it play!"

In the myth, written in about 2300 BCE, Inanna descends into the underworld to face her sister who is grieving the recent death of her husband. She passes through seven gates as she descends and is stripped at each one of her crown, royal robe, jewels, breast plate, hip girdle, bracelets, and gold rings. Naked, she faces Ereshkigal, who is neither a quiet nor solitary griever. She wails, moans, screeches, and keels. Not feeling like Inanna is doing enough to share her grief, she fastens on Inanna "the eye of death," turns her into rotting green meat, and hangs her on a meat hook where she remains for three days before being rescued so she can return to Earth. Lots of similarity to the Jesus story that was written a few thousand years after Inanna.

Olympia invites us each day to feel the Inanna story, allow the details to resonate through our bodies. The actresses redirect us, often and always, out of our brains and into our bodies. Olympia invites our inner "fools" to come out of hiding, have some fun.

"Move, moan, dance, cry your heart out just like Ereshkigal and Inanna," Olympia instructs. And do not be afraid to cry, she tells us, with a line that sticks with me: "Your tears are a river through, so get in your boat and row!"

On the final day, trust runs deep among us all. We each draw slips of paper from a basket with phrases quoted from the translation of Inanna's myth: "You are a woman who decides the fate of the land." "You are a woman who has known betrayal and survival."

One by one, we draw our cue and stand in the center of the room, all eyes watching and supportive, to see what our bodies have to say. The toxic fumes of shame and guilt, lodged inside our bodies by notions of sin, show up that day. Inanna has a thing or two to teach us about ridding our bodies of sin's toxicity.

"Let sounds come out of you; keep moving," Olympia urges, again and again.

Celia draws the first slip and reads out loud: "You are a woman who knows shame." Forty-four sets of eyes stare at her, supportive and caring. The morning breeze whispers through the pines just outside the screens. Celia does not move to the center of the circle as had been suggested. Her shame roots her in place. She wears a floor-length skirt and strappy black sandals with jet-black hair that curls below her shoulders. She slowly dips down, grasps the hem of her skirt, and inches it up her right leg which juts out toward the center of our circle. Her bare thigh, for all of us to see.

"My shame," she states in a clear, calm voice.

We hold silence as we behold her full-fleshed thigh. Her shame is our own shame in at least one body part. Thighs, stomachs, hips, breasts too large or small. Female body-shame is a shared birthright.

Celia does not need to move or say a word. Her exposed thigh says it all.

My turn comes late in the afternoon. I draw a phrase describing Ereshkigal: "You are a woman who utters the cry of guilt."

I take my place in the center of the circle trying to conjure "guilt." Dressed in a long lacy black dress with tights and a leotard beneath, the afternoon sun streams through the skylight, warms my long brown hair on my back. I feel not a hint of guilt, just a warm glow from the week-long journey.

"I wasn't raised Catholic," I joke as I stand, stock still, in the middle of the circle of women, waiting for guilt to arrive. "I don't really do much guilt."

Olympia is not buying my denial. "Stay with it," she tells me. "No words, just move and see what comes up."

I walk slowly inside the large circle of women, close my eyes, and let my energy sink down into my body as I zig-zag from one side of the circle to the other. Nothing.

I draw my eyes into slits like I had as child in the elm tree, blending the women, the hexagonal-screened room and the oceans of green trees outside the windows into a whole.

"It's in your teeth," Olympia says. "I see it in your teeth."

Her words stop me cold. My hand instinctively flies to my mouth and tears flow. My mother had large, beautiful, protruding front teeth, which I adored. Never self-conscious about them, her smile stretched extra wide. When Olympia notices energy in my teeth, floods of guilt and grief surge inside of me.

My guilt, which I had repressed for fifteen years, took root inside me on the afternoon I left Mom on the couch, crippled, to fly back to Washington. It flourished seven months later when I did not take an earlier flight and arrived after she was put under anesthesia for her brain surgery. We could have had one last conversation, me holding her hand telling her how much I loved her. Instead, I had just started a new job and needed to finish a newsletter, so I reserved a later flight that landed me in San Bernardino too late. Mom never woke up after surgery and then lay in a coma of silence for eleven days before dying.

I start to explain but Olympia stops me.

"Don't talk, move. What does guilt feel like and sound like? Let us hear it, see it."

I tilt my head toward the skylight, spread arms wide, and open my mouth wide to gulp in sunlight, turning round and round. Guilt bubbles up from my moving body and grows into a wail, bereft and anguished, barreling toward sobs.

"Her teeth," I say through my tears. "How did you know?"

Olympia does not answer.

No one says a word. No one offers interpretations or hugs. They simply hold the space.

When the session ends that afternoon, all of us spent from the strong emotions we had shared and witnessed, we hug and cry together.

"My mother has buck teeth," one of the women whispers to me. "I won't be embarrassed of them ever again." I give her a big hug.

I feel strengthened, not vulnerable. Cleansed. Fresh and new.

Olympia believes in mystery. She has eyes and ears that see and hear, beneath and beyond, and she helps each of us discover that we do too. Open your eyes, ears, and heart. Move, breathe, and claim it all.

Olympia teaches me how to pray. She never makes that claim but I learn from her that prayer works best when it engages the whole of my body and soul. No clasped hands, hard pews, tightly crossed legs as I struggle for the right words at Del Rosa Methodist Church. Prayer is movement and sound and sweat and tears, mixed and tumbled, an umbilical connection to all of nature. Prayers pulse my body, soul, and spirit as one.

Dear Father,

I sit by your side as you lay dying in our living room on Mountain Avenue in San Bernardino. November 1993, just four months after my journey to Inanna. Dawn comes as you take your exit. The day before you die, I sit beside your unconscious body in a hospital bed in the living room on Mountain Avenue. For hours, I tell you family stories and play your favorite 1940s music which, I hope, carries you back to the days and nights you wooed our mother, dead now for fifteen years. The woman you love utterly and completely.

Dear, dear Father, you will always be my blueprint for Other. I know how hard you struggled to earn enough money to feed and house all seven of us, and I know the pain of your own early life when you wanted so much for your own father to love you as much as you thought he loved your older brother and younger sister. I'll-Show-You filled in the deep chip on your shoulders.

Do you know the I'll-Show-You spirit I learned from you fuels my own strength to take on authority, question what I have been taught. You modeled the courage I need to unearth my own soul and spirit. I'll-Show-You is the lifeblood of my rogue.

You were unconscious for twenty-four hours but that morning, just before dawn, your blue eyes open wide. I sit closest to your head, holding your left hand, all of us siblings circled round. You peer into my eyes and then look over my left shoulder and spot something, someone. Mom? Your parents? I have no idea but I know you have gotten the signal to come on over, the water's fine. Your eyes look one last time into mine before you shut them for good.

You were a good Dad, I whisper as I stroke his hand, and let him go. Death is a sacred passage, intimate and intense, and I am awed by my father's courage in facing death, straight on, accepting death with solemn strength.

Dad modeled spunk, impatience, and ambition. A human father, imperfect, whose flaws taught me as much as his love. *I'll show you, Dad. I will still show you,* I whisper to his now-empty body, praying his rogue energy stays with me in my now fatherless world.

REIGNING MEN

When women act like women, they are accused of being inferior.
When women act like human beings, they are
accused of behaving like men.

—Simone de Beauvoir, *The Second Sex*

Dear Money,

I thought you would be proud that I got myself through graduate school, found work as a psychotherapist, and completed a winter program on dream analysis at the C.G. Jung Institute in Zurich. I was making marriage work with Peter. And, oh yes, I ran a marathon. I'm not bragging here, you judger of worth, but I struggle with why you couldn't let me be.

You sniff the tug inside of me between soul-work and money-work. You see an opening and whisper in my ear: Hey, little one. You could make a lot more money as a lobbyist. Do you really want to spend your days listening to people's problems?

You know Times Mirror, where I have been consulting during graduate school, is about to dangle a sweet offer: director of the Washington, DC, office, triple-digit salary, annual bonus, stock options, and excellent health care benefits.

You slither in, serpentine, hissing in my ear: big job, big

money, prestige, come on little girl, claim your place in the
nation's top 1 percent of female wage earners.

   I drop to my knees more than once and beg to be shown
the way. And you, money, answer me the loudest. Money: the
ruling God of Washington, DC, the purchaser of power and
prestige. You glitter and gleam when they dangle you.

   I say yes.

Men-gods wear suits, well-tailored, crisp white shirts, and ties
in shades of blue and red, an occasional pink or yellow. They smell
of aftershave and real leather. Conference tables are their command
centers and limos their drive of choice. They wear expensive slip-on
shoes, shiny browns and blacks that look to be buffed daily, hourly.
No scuffs dare sully their shiny surface.

   I paint God on their faces and vest in them all power and authority. They are the ones to whom I offer prayers to hire me, grant me
high-paying jobs. They are the ones before whom I humble myself, flirt,
and try always to sound smart. The ones for whom I spend thousands
of dollars on DKNY clothing, haircuts, creams, nail polishes, perfumes,
and high-quality mascara that dramatize my eyes, lengthen my lashes.

   In my early days as a lobbyist, a media mogul offers me a ride in
his limo after a business dinner. I do not want to go, and had neither
flirted nor betrayed a hint of interest. I am not yet thirty, in the flush
of my beauty that is pasted over innards that are unrooted and afraid.
He favors young beauty shellacked atop insecurity.

   "Do I have to go with him?" I ask my friend, a high-level First
Amendment lawyer thirty years my senior whom I like and trust.

   "Absolutely not," he answers quickly, but still I wonder whether
a "no" will harm my future job success or a "yes" might grant me a
better career.

I say no, but why did I have to ask another's opinion? I knew that "no" bone deep.

My beauty is a shepherd that leads me into dangerous waters and betrays my soul. Female beauty and brokenness, when mixed, create a toxic cocktail that should be called a Marilyn, served straight up, shaken and twisted.

The fallacy of painting God on men's faces, imagining them to be gods, becomes clear to me in my forties on a warm summer evening in Los Angeles in the backyard of the publisher of the *Los Angeles Times*. We sit at a long dining table, the backyard strung with twinkly white lights. I am the only woman at the table along with ten executives from Times Mirror–owned newspapers.

As head of Times Mirror's Washington, DC, office, I lobby on behalf of the media owned by Times Mirror, which includes newspapers, broadcast and cable stations, books, and magazines. Director was my title, the first woman to head the office but also the first one in the position who somehow did not deserve the title of vice president, which my two predecessors, both male, had been granted without question. By this time, my self-assurance had risen but still I work in a world of men I vest with power that I should claim for myself.

On that night, lights sparkling, wine flowing, Mr. CEO sits in his big chair at the head of the table with all the male publishers and me arranged around him. Their neckties, blue, red, and two yellows, knot noose-like around their throats. No matter they are drinking wine that should have relaxed them, even though it is warm and I know they long to loosen ties from their executive necks, they do not because there sits Mr. CEO at the head of the table with his tie knotted beneath his chin.

More than an hour into the evening, well past appetizers and salad and halfway into grilled lamb and fresh asparagus, Mr. CEO unlooses his tie in a swift, two-handed gesture: one hand on the knot while his other hand tugs at the back tail of the tie, a gentle nudge and, ahhh, free. Mr. CEO also unbuttons the top button of his shirt with an extra tug, picks up his wine glass (he owns a winery you know), and sips his expensive red.

This is the moment my men-as-Gods obsession crumbles. Only when Mr. CEO unknots his tie and unbuttons his top button do twenty hands, simultaneously, make their way to knots and buttons, unloose in perfect sync their necks from knotted grips, and release deep exhales of collective relief as they sip their wine.

I see a truth in this tableau of manhood: A handful of Alpha males, fat with ego, rise to the top on the backs of all the lower dogs who know they are not Alpha, but excel, brilliantly and willingly, at riding Alpha coattails. Not a rogue in sight. What my eyes had seen could never be unseen. I pick up my wine and raise my glass ever so slightly toward the glittery LA night sky to toast my own powers of mystery and sight. I know, full well, the ties that bind my female life but am grateful to be spared neckties of control.

◉

Big jolts of Sky-God energy—all-powerful and superior to the masses—fuels me when I buy a new car. Everyone out of my way. I own this world. It's mine.

Not just any car: A brand-new teal-green eight-cylinder five-speed Mustang GT. I walk into the dealership one Saturday after-noon and slap down my money. Okay, not actual cash but a fat check. I buy that baby with no hesitation. I know what I want, and I want it bad. The rush is immediate. My body pumps me full of a raw sense of entitlement and power, what has to be what a testosterone rush feels like. Move over, out of the way, I'm here now and I've got keys.

I had been driving a Geo Metro for several years before buying the Mustang. The Metro had, maybe, one cylinder, that made me sweat every time I made a left-hand turn, certain oncoming traffic even when three blocks away would ram into me as I madly pumped the gas.

The Mustang delivers. I tuck in behind the wheel, adjust my sunglasses in the rearview mirror, primp my hair, reapply dark red lipstick, and put pedal to the metal. There is no place in that car for vulnerability or insecurity. The V-8 engine purrs in harmony with my body, rendering me oblivious to danger and even death. I look hot. The car is hot. All I want from anyone else is their jealous drool.

The swan song of my Mustang years is a solo road trip cross-country from Washington, DC, to New Mexico and back. Me, behind the wheel, passing truckers on open roads across Louisiana, my long brown hair streaming behind me as they honk and wave. When I hit the Texas border, where the speed limit leaps to eighty-five mph, I pop Lyle Lovett into the CD player, crank it loud, and floor it all the way across Texas's broad belly and big sky. The wind at my back, a full tank of gas. Pumped, primed, and arrogant.

◉

Exhausted after a long day at work, I draw a hot bubble bath to soak my soul back to life. That night, in my sea of bubbles, my nipples poke above the surface, pink tips on white foam. Candles flicker near my head and Bach's Piano Concerto in F Minor plays in the background. I take a deep breath and release it slowly as the hot water softens my skin.

I close my eyes and lean my head against the rim of the tub. Trying not to think about work, I look down at my breasts among the bubbles, and the thought of my lunch that day with male colleagues interrupts my candlelight.

My breasts became a topic in our lunchtime banter when one of the men dubbed mine "tweeners." For the record, he had neither seen nor touched them.

"Not too big and not too small," Trib-Guy said with a wink. He had been describing another woman's breasts when he felt compelled to label mine. All three of the men are friends and maybe Trib-Guy is being kind, trying to be inclusive? They laughed at the comment, and I cloaked my anger inside a chuckle, a talent at which I excel due to my many years in the business world. Me, offended? Nah. I'm just one of the guys.

We are all highly paid lobbyists in Washington, DC, and I had learned how to button down my anger at the sexism that rears its head with astonishing regularity. It is the 1990s in the male-dominated world of our nation's capital. I bulk up each morning in shoulder-padded business jackets that offer little protection from the daily gridiron tactics and locker room banter. I stared down at my overpriced salmon and wild rice that tweener-guy paid for with his expense account.

What's the sin in this? It was a joke. Lighten up.

My bath water cools so I turn on the hot water and add another splash of bubbles. As I look at my body immersed in water, the answer to my long-held question—*What's the sin in this?*—bolts out of me, full-bodied and alive, like Athena sprung from the head of Zeus: *There is no sin in this. There is no sin in my body. There is no sin in me.*

No sin, I know as I look down at my breasts, run a hand over my belly. "There is no sin in my female body!" I shout loud enough that my words echo off the bathroom walls.

I draw in a deep breath, dunk my head beneath the surface of the water, baptize my sin-free body. My body feels light and free as I release the leaden weight. I hold my breath as long as I can, surface, gulp air, and dunk two more times for good measure. One each for the confines of three-dimensional life where culture controls and monetizes female bodies while fourth-dimensional mystery, accessed through dreams and intuition, languishes in the background, waiting for us to wake up.

There is no sin in my female body. I feel the absolute rightness of this just like I felt goosebumps of grace as a child in the limbs of our elm tree. The truth of "no such thing as sin" resonates through my every pore: No sin. No question. Mic drop.

⊙

I am guilty, many times over, again and again, of bestowing god-like authority on men in my life. Boyfriends, bosses, political leaders, teachers, father, and friends. So much smarter than me, more politically astute, never more moral or a bigger heart, but what does that count for anyway?

I want them to be gods. I need them to know all, to know me better than I know myself. See me. Save me. During my teen years I madly paste God's face on boys: love me, notice me. During my adult years I pray they realize how smart I am with all my degrees: hire me, promote me.

It's not all my fault. Images of God and Jesus saturate our world, fuel our inclination to paint God faces on men. Holy, holy, holy. The multitude of graven images of God as a white male make it a simple leap to paint God faces on men.

You know how I get better? I find inside myself what I wasted long years searching for outside. It's that simple. I quit searching for divinity in men's faces when I found it inside my own body and heart, on sandy beaches, mountain ridges, chill mountain lakes, and arid desert landscapes. I claim the elemental divinity of nature that is there for me every day when I sit quietly and slurp it in.

I can only imagine that stripping god masks off men frees them up to be human just as letting women step down from pedestals of goodness and purity allows us to be simply human. No masks needed. A host of broken, struggling humans trying to do our best.

> *Dear Corporate America,*
>
> *You do not make it easy for a woman walking your hallowed halls. Do you know how hard we try to fit in, be heard, sound smart? Female rogues are, decidedly, unwelcome. Do you know how carefully we couch our words in ways palatable to your ears. Emotion-free? Rational. Logical. Do you realize we know we have bodies but we also know how to play them up and play them down, coat our faces in makeup, and paint our nails blood red.*
>
> *Why do you want such a small percentage of my talents?*
>
> *Imagine a world where the whole of every female is invited to show up with instinct, intellect, and intuition in high gear. Here's the truth: All my good behavior and quality output never trumps my femaleness.*

My boss, a senior vice president based in our corporate offices in Los Angeles, calls me on a Tuesday afternoon. I sit at my desk in my big office with its couch, two chairs, my own television set, and expensive modern art on the walls. From my eleventh-floor perch, I can see the National Cathedral, glimmering like Oz, up Wisconsin Avenue. I am wearing a ruby-red jacket which I recall vividly because I spot a small bit of lint on the sleeve on which I fixate as we speak.

I am three years into my position as director of the Washington, DC, office. On that day, me in DC and he in LA, I make the case that I deserve a vice president title. I had recently made a presentation on the White House lawn to President Clinton. The event had been covered by CNN and C-Span and there I was on the national news, telling the president about wireless technology, getting great press for our company, looking beautiful, confident, well-informed.

"I feel like I have earned the VP title," I state clearly after citing my achievements.

Mr. SVP is quiet for a moment. "You have been doing a very good job," he tells me. I knew a "but" was next up. It is a doozy.

"You know we have three women at the corporate director level in Los Angeles. If we promote you to VP, we would have to promote all of them too."

It is my turn to be quiet for a moment. Here's where my ability to tamp down emotions in the corporate world came in handy. Rage floods my body. I'm yoked to three other women just because of gender? I think to myself, *They have hit their vagina quota.*

"Seriously?" is the word I manage. What I didn't say: *Do you know how big the lawsuit could be if I were recording this call?*

"I am sorry," he says. "You are doing a great job. But my hands are tied."

I swallow my rage and hang up the phone. A lawsuit would be expensive, take many months, and blackball any corporate future. Deep breath in. Swallow feelings. Deep breath out. Smile. And so I did.

Two years later, a new CEO is on board. He has been hired to facilitate the sale of Times Mirror to the Tribune Company. The Tribune Company has its own Washington, DC, corporate office so the office I run is on the chopping block.

The SVP flies to Washington to tell me in person they are closing us all down. The buyout he offers for my director-level position is six months of salary and benefits. After I have a few days to chew on it, I call Mr. SVP and tell him I was denied the VP promotion because I had been yoked to three other women in corporate. It is unfair, I tell him, calmly, to be cheated out of a VP level buyout because of that litigious fact. I lay out my position clearly, emotion-free. He says he will get back to me. A few days later he calls and offers a year of full salary and benefits and six months beyond that as a consultant to the company.

A wise bumper sticker once told me: If you want peace, work for justice. My boss's offer feels like a modicum of justice. A sense of peace trickles through my body, and I do nothing at all to tamp it down.

THE DESERT

The desert has its own music.

—Mary Austin, *The Land of Little Rains*

WE LIVE CLOSE ENOUGH to the Pentagon that our windows shake when American Airlines Flight 77 crashes into its walls on September 11, 2001. A few months later, a sniper stalks our region, murdering one man as he pumps gas at a station near our home and another in the Home Depot parking lot where Peter often goes on Saturdays.

Our front room has two large windows open to the street. When I read on the couch I sink as deeply as I can into the couch pillows, holding the book close to my nose so the sniper cannot see me if he drives down our street looking for someone to kill.

Fear is not the only motivation for our move. We had lived in the big city for nearly thirty years and are ready for a change. Tucson, Arizona, is on our radar because two of my brothers live in Phoenix, about two hours away; the University of Arizona is in Tucson; and I had just read *High Tide in Tucson* by Barbara Kingsolver. It didn't take much. We are ready for new geography.

We book a flight in June 2002, eight months after they nabbed the sniper, and land in the middle of 108-degree weather. No matter. We know no one in town but fall in love instantly with quail families skittering between mesquite trees, the enormous sky, and the bracelet of mountains surrounding the city that remind me of the San Bernardino Valley that grew me.

Peter and I are in full agreement about making the big move. Bada-boom-bada-bing, in what seems like two breaths, Peter offers himself up for a buyout from National Public Radio where he was executive producer of *Talk of the Nation*. I quit my job as communications director for the National Osteoporosis Foundation. We sell our house, move to Tucson, buy a house, and arrive in our new lives jobless and excited.

Rita is among the first friends I meet in Tucson. She had trained in Africa on the art of throwing bones, an African version of Tarot cards. In a one-on-one session, she throws sticks not bones that deliver a clear message: "You have been sent to Tucson for a reason," she tells me. "You were picked up by the scruffs of your necks and plopped here because there is something you need to learn."

Turns out, I, more than Peter, have much to learn. Curiosity about desert life draws me to the Sonoran landscape: lizards and prickly pear, coyotes and bougainvillea, dry river beds and snow-covered mountains awaken parts of me deadened by male statues on every corner in Washington, DC, and left empty by the giant penile-obelisk honoring President George Washington in the center of the mall. Grandmother Saguaro to the rescue.

I had not been consciously aware of how much my soul and spirit are in need of time to wander and wonder through the desert. The Sonoran Desert, I discover, challenges even as it slowly reveals what I need to let go of, burn out of me. Change never comes easy.

In this arid land, I will be hit on, shoved out, shot at, and treated like dirt. The slings and arrows of patriarchy are as abundant as prickly pear in the Sonoran Desert. I take on a one-star General, retired, who espouses decency and honor while urging me to lie. A lusting chancellor who fancies himself Sun Tzu and we, his employees, the enemy. A host of old white men with not a rogue among them who follow these "leaders" with tight ties and blind obedience. And a woman, who drank the patriarchal Kool-Aid and fires me for excelling on the job because, she tells me, it made her look bad in front of the board.

"What are you going to tell the board?" I ask her the day she fires me, knowing my track record is excellent and the board respects my talents.

"Can I tell them you quit?" she asks.

"No. You cannot."

The desert is the breeding ground for reclaiming my rogue. Desert geography mirrors strength from cacti, sun, and stretches of wild land directly to my DNA. As I move from job to job, my desert-rogue energy awakens. What I do for work and how much I am paid no longer drive me. I am plopped into the desert to reclaim soul and spirt, neither of which are available for purchase. Visions of whole, horny, happy, and holy in my female body drive me forward.

Dear Grandmother Saguaro,

Your beauty stops my heart. A beacon of hope in the Sonoran Desert. I am barely into my fifties when we move to the desert, the same age as you when you grow arms. Your beauty and heft comfort. So mighty. Two hundred years can be your life span, eighty feet your height, and several tons your weight. Formidable! You do not disappoint.

Your sacredness is honored by the Tohono O'odham, Native Americans who first settled this land and still live here today. They hold as most holy your strength and beauty. You begin your long life as sprouts beneath a "nurse tree," usually a Palo Verde, ironwood, or mesquite. You survive the desert heat in your young years because they provide shade so you can grow strong enough to handle the heat on your own. Nature's brilliance. As you continue to grow, these much older trees may die off.

Your beauty, not unlike life, comes with sharp needles, breathtaking but short-lived blossoms, and a tough hide. You hold the power to survive drought, extreme heat, holes bored into your belly by Gila woodpeckers, and humans sporting arrows and guns who selfishly view you as targets.

Dear Grandmother Saguaro, you are my nurse tree. I cannot lean into you like I did my elm but I often stand at your side, gaze up at your towering presence, and am humbled, awed. Divinity incarnate. Ancient wisdom rooted in endurance and resilience. A graven image of female holy that warms and comforts my heart.

Elise is the first person I meet in Tucson. She is introduced to me by Jane, a friend in Atlanta whom I met at a workshop in Abiquiu, New Mexico, who met Elise at a workshop in Taos. A friendship that defies this much geography is meant to be. Jane introduces Elise and me over the phone and our friendship sparks. Elise hosts a monthly group in Tucson known as The Well, in honor of women in ancient days who met at community wells to draw water for drinking and bathing but also to tell secrets, share stories, dreams, and pain. She invites me to join her group soon after we land in Tucson.

We meet monthly, ten to fifteen of us, sitting on chairs and a sofa circled round Elise's living room with gorgeous views of the Catalina Mountains.

The Well gifts me Mary Magdalene.

Elise was raised a preacher's daughter in Texas, and earned her PhD in Mythological Studies from Pacifica Graduate Institute near Santa Barbara, CA. Her dissertation included research on Mary Magdalene. Elise also studied at the Jungian Institute in Zurich. Dreams, mythology, and Mary Magdalene cement our friendship.

Another dear friendship that blossoms at The Well is with Mary Beth, who has a doctorate in higher education. She was raised in Detroit by a rabid Catholic mother and struggled against rigid rules about sexuality and faith.

Organized religion has let all three of us down but spiritual curiosity burns deep within each of us, solders us into a beautiful whole.

We share stories about the virgin-whore tightrope we have all been forced to find our way across. A tightrope strung by early church leaders.

"How do we snuff out female holy?" I imagine ancient church leaders asking each other. "Every last ounce of it," I can hear them saying. "So let's elevate virgins and brandish the slut label with all our might."

Mary Magdalene bore the brunt of the deadly slut label. In fact, she plays one of the lead slut roles in female history. Despite her holy alliance with Jesus. Despite her talent in visioning and her profound belief and understanding of Jesus's teachings. Slut is how she is best remembered.

Mary Magdalene. Say her name.

As I child, I notice how her name drowns in tsk-tsks whenever it floats down from the pulpit at Del Rosa Methodist. Wanton, purveyor of sin. *A prostitute, you know,* they whisper behind their hymnals. Unlike the love that lilts from mouths when speaking of the good Mary, Mother of Jesus. Black-white, sinner-saint. Two stark choices are all the church offers as divine female role models.

The Well gatherings, and Elise's research, inspire me to read The Gospel of Mary Magdalene, one of the Gospels written circa 300 AD that had been banished, destroyed, and buried by renegade monks. Mary's Gospel, which remained hidden until 1896 and was not translated and published until 1955, paints a different picture of Christ and his teachings than the Gospels in the Bible. Her Jesus preaches love within the hearts of all living entities. Animal, mineral, flora, and fauna all sprung from the same cells. No outside blessings required.

My research leads me to a shape-shifting, rogue-inspiring truth: *Mary Magdalene was not a slut.* She was the holiest of the holy. She "got" what Jesus was teaching and lived divine spirit and vision from the inside out.

In fact, the Catholic Church in 1969 acknowledged Mary Magdalene was not a prostitute, and in 2016 designated her as Apostle to the Apostles. (They could not go so far as to name her a full-fledged Apostle.) But they admitted Mary Magdalene was *not* a wanton woman. They agreed she had eyes and a heart that could see and feel beneath and beyond our three-dimensional world. She was master of vision, sacred touch, and anointing, and is credited in the Gospel of John as the first witness of the arisen Jesus. The Queen of Sight and Vision.

"All nature, all formations, all creatures exist in and with one another . . . He who has ears to hear, let him hear," Mary's Gospel reads. I had known as a child, body-deep, my shared connection with elm, sky, and mountains. Mary's words resonate with truth inside me.

The passage that stops me cold is the question posed to me in my dream years earlier: "What's the sin in this?"

In Mary's Gospel, the Apostles are meeting with Jesus when Peter poses the question: "Then Peter said to Jesus: 'You have been explaining every topic to us; tell us one thing. What is the sin of the world?' The Savior replied, 'There is no such thing as sin.'

There is no such thing as sin. The morning I stumble on this passage I am dressed to go running. The answer jumps off the page and smacks me in the face. I run to find my dream journal to be sure of the details. There it is: the Jewish woman with the ancient pot asking me nearly the same question that Peter poses to Jesus. *What is the sin of the world? What's the sin in this?* And Jesus's answer? *There is no such thing as sin.* The same answer my body provided in my bubble bath epiphany.

When the question was first asked of me in my dream more than twenty years earlier, I had no clue the Gospel of Mary Magdalene existed. All I knew of Mary Magdalene was her alleged wanton ways. Like my shibboleth dream, "What's the sin in this" bolts straight out of the collective unconscious, the vast archetypal experiences of humans throughout time including love, hate, marriage, murder, and God. And oh yes, sin. The new truth about this ancestral DNA springs to life my DNA, a game changer of new possibilities, new ways of integrating and claiming my own sexuality as divine.

The libel of Mary Magdalene froze my DNA in the hamster loop of virgin-whore. Ancient trauma that took my female sexuality hostage. As I reread the line several times, I swear I feel my DNA shifting and opening inside of me, slurping in this ancient, inherited truth: *There is no such thing as sin.* Mary Magdalene's Gospel turns my DNA toward the light of vision, anointing, touch, and sin-free bodies. My body tingles with the new information. The truth.

That morning, my run has to wait. I have my answer, translated and printed in black and white. *There's no such thing as sin.* My discovery whets my curiosity to learn all I can about Mary Magdalene. Not just through reading and research, but as Olympia taught, by feeling, breathing, and reimagining Mary Magdalene in my body, my life.

◉

Elise and Mary Beth and I meet weekly to write at Bentley's, a local coffeehouse close to the University of Arizona. The walls are decorated with funky art from local artists. The coffee is excellent and their homemade bran muffins melt in your mouth.

We all have our journals and at least two pens each.

"You guys ready for this?" I ask Elise and Mary Beth the first day we settle in to right our worlds by writing.

"I'm kinda afraid of lightning," Mary Beth jokes, knowing we will be imagining and capturing on paper new images of female divinity and sexuality.

In a world where female visions and voices have been erased for centuries, the three of us are eager to set our imaginations free. Reimagine the tired stories and lies. No church dogma or creed to reign us in. We are eager to get to the writing. I can almost feel my imagination like a snorting stallion inside of me eager for release, expression. Bentley's is quiet this morning, the only sound is the chug of a coffee pot behind the counter and our scribbling pens.

Over the next few months, our pens wander through the thickets of female divinity. We wander with our words beyond Mary Magdalene to reimagine Eve and Mary.

◉

Eve bites into that ripe red apple with a loud crunch, her teeth unloosing droplets of juice that moisten her lips, trickle down her chin. She closes her eyes, savoring the apple's tart flesh.

In that split second between her first bite and God's wrathful response, she is alive, hungry, and basking in nature. For that instant, Eve marvels at the wondrous fruit, feels its flesh against her teeth, drinks down the juice. Sin does not flow immediately from the tree-grown apple to Eve's body, but sin's slimy fingers are poised, ready.

Until that fateful moment, Eve strode strong across the land of Eden, comfortable in her passion, wet with God-created lust. She was alive, voracious, naked, curious in a female body that mirrored the beauty of Eden.

Did God pause for a moment here? Did he allow Eve to savor the entire apple? Did he beam with pride that Eve's wondrous body could produce whole humans just like he did Adam and Eve? Did God pause for a moment before sliming Eve's female body with sin or did he, without hesitation or thought, cast Eve from Eden after just one bite?

I imagine a tiny sliver of apple-flesh lodged in Eve's back teeth. As God thunders and curses, Eve finds the sliver with her tongue, rolls it around her mouth, imprints the sensation on her body. She whispers this memory into ears that can hear: *walk the earth in female form with pride and courage. You need not be lassoed nor trussed. You are divine.*

⊙

The dark bush of Mary's vagina grows toward her navel and along her inner thighs. Sturdy thighs, dimpled and strong enough to birth the baby Jesus. Her vagina pulses the night God implants his seed. She spreads her legs wide with a resounding yes, just yes, oh yes. Her vagina drips liquid moist and wet, her clitoris swells and soars, coaxed by her own fingers, which play also with her nipples. Spread warm and wide, every hair of her body awake and alive. Her heart pounds from the magic that goes down that night. Her body.

Nine months Jesus lay in her belly, his Prince-of-God feet hammering from the inside, nurtured by and breathing the warm wet of her. Nine months from the early spring plowing to the crystalline darkness of a December night.

On that night, oh what a night, blood stains the hay and splatters the donkeys and lambs. Mary's screams pierce the starry night. She will not let this one out easy.

"Go away," she screams at Joseph, who stands helpless at her side all night long as Mary moans, pushes, bleeds, and sweats.

"He's mine," she says, spitting at Joseph who knows not what to do.

Jesus remains stuck between womb and the world. He is in no hurry to enter a life in which thorns will be planted on his head, swords plunged in his side, and nails hammered through his palms on a cross where he will die, tethered in pain.

Finally, Mary pushes him out and lies spent, her dark hair matted, spittle on cheeks and chin, and blood, everywhere blood.

"Hurry," Joseph says. "Clean up. The Magi will soon be here."

Mary holds Jesus to her breast and glares at Joseph.

"Piss off," she hisses. "This is my time, my blood and sweat." She lies back, Jesus swaddled safe against her chest, and listens to the mournful hum of her now-empty womb.

The chill stable air shivers her body. She presses her cheek against her new baby's still-damp head, savors the breath, blood, and flesh of him, hoarding the seconds she has before being forced to cede full custody to God the Father who lives in the sky.

◉

The Sonoran Desert teaches me the stench of sexual harassment on my female skin. Covert sexual harassment was part of my everyday diet during my Washington, DC, years: jokes, winks, talking over me, the rage when my knowledge is ignored until a man at the long conference table repeats what I say and is nodded at and praised for his wisdom. I deal with it. But overt sexual harassment? A whole different beast.

The Sonoran Desert insists I feel and process the full impact of harassment on my body, self, and soul. Harassment is an ancient art that is as accepted for males as virginity is for females. The birth rite of patriarchy just as virginity is the birthright of powerless females.

Why am I surprised when harassment slimes my body in Tucson? The foundations of harassment are pounce and surprise. Woo them with mentoring. Praise their brains and smarts. Promise advancement. Pounce. Surprise is central to the experience.

In those first seconds, split seconds, the world bifurcates into before and after. Time and reality melt and seep like hot lava beneath my skin, my breath stops breathing. I stand unprotected: no shell, no fur, no needles, no armor. Sweat rises on my palms. My heart pounds and belly reels as he leers at my outsides.

I want to bolt out of his office, out of my job. He is the boss of me so I freeze my face into a blank stare as he morphs from boss to enemy, leader to predator, trusted to abusive.

Inhale denial. Exhale rage. Stand statue-like as dread courses through you. Remain silent. Rage can, absolutely, not be expressed. No matter how justified. Rage must be swallowed, buried deep in belly and thighs, where it sits and rots for years.

He brandishes poetry and love songs that clash with the memos on his desk. *Ode to a Nude* by Pablo Neruda tumbles from his mouth as he sits in front of bookshelves lined with theories of higher education. He is chancellor of the local community college. Hear him roar.

Your breasts of level plentitude, fulfilled by living light, he reads, leering up at me where I stand, on the other side of the desk, stunned and staring, my face a frozen mask.

Even more naked, he telephones me in the office from his bath-tub, water splashing, *oops I dropped the soap*, affirming his naked-ness as he talks about an upcoming committee meeting. I stare at the Catalina Mountains outside my office window. Disgusted.

His behavior is too egregious to defuse with humor. Legions beyond "tweeners." He touts words of his god, Sun Tzu, who wrote *The Art of War* that teaches prayers of dominance: "Let your plans be dark and impenetrable as night, and when you move, fall like a thunderbolt."

He thunderbolts through many women's careers, men's too but with cruelty not sex, ripping holes in lives and livelihoods. Of course, he denies every shred. Eight of us come forward with stories of his sexual harassment matching in theme and detail but they rule no proof, no witnesses, not within the statute of limitations.

Ah, the statute of limitations. A brick wall of legality built by men to enable their harassing behavior. A brick wall that obliterates female rights and dashes female careers, hopes, and dreams. Hard red concrete that bricks in female lives while enabling men to deny their behavior, pretend it away, shove it into their past, go forth, and do it again.

My harasser rides out of town with a massive severance package while we, his victims, are left with the gnawing anger of injustice, lower salaries, dead-end jobs, and broken trust. Of course, they believe him not us. The women outnumber the man eight to one but those odds are not good enough. The She stands alone when man-handled by godless gods.

The stink of injustice remains in my heart, turns cartwheels in my stomach, betrayed as I am not just by my boss but by the system and culture. My skin still prickles when I hear the harasser's name or the names of the lawyers who protected him.

This trauma is mine forever.

HARD STOP

Pain nourishes courage. You can't be brave if you've only had won-derful things happen to you.

—Mary Tyler Moore

THE BULLETS FIRE and stop, and my friends lay bloody and dead on the concrete of Safeway in Tucson, Arizona. I stare down at them slumped on the ground and know I cannot help. My blood pressure pumps wildly, fills my muscles for flight, but there is no escape.

In those first seconds of horror and confusion, my body, with cool logic, takes charge. An internal cacophony of spitting hormones, throbbing veins, and speeding heart even as I freeze in place. My peripheral vision vanishes, and my nose and eyes refuse to smell or see the blood-covered concrete. My blood-covered friends. My ears block out moans and the sounds of hands pounding against chests to make hearts beat again. I desperately want my friends unbloody, undead.

People strap my arm with blood pressure cuffs, again and again, drape blankets around me and say, drink water, drink water, again and again and again. I do whatever anyone tells me to do. Fire engines, police cars, ambulances, and helicopters swoop into the scene and treat and tend and save and pronounce dead. I hear only silence.

Thirty-three bullets, 19:06 seconds. Thirteen wounded and six dead, ranging in age from nine to sixty-nine, at the constituent event of Congresswoman Gabrielle Giffords, who represented Southern Arizona and for whom I had worked for one and a half years as her director of community outreach. Congress on Your Corner is hosted by Gabby to connect directly with her constituents. The gunman who shows up that day seeks murder not conversation. He stands in the exact spot where I had been seconds earlier. He aims his Glock at Congresswoman Giffords's head at 10:12 a.m., and I watch from a few feet away as he spews bullets into Gabby, my former boss, and several other dear friends, killing one of them.

The shooting takes place on January 8, 2011, the second Saturday of the New Year. Three days earlier I dreamt of a giant explosion at the University of Arizona. In my dream windows shattered around me when a nearby campus building was bombed. My body shook with the building but I realized I was alive. *Everything has changed*, I thought to myself in the dream. *Everything has changed.*

Moments after the Safeway shooting, I sit on a small ledge outside the store, rocking, arms wrapped around my terrified body, repeating, "I dreamt this, I dreamt this," my body shaking with terror. "Those are my friends. Everything has changed, everything has changed." My body rocks to the rhythm of the words, desperate for comfort.

After the gunman is tackled and the bullets stop, I am told to stay at the scene with other witnesses. We amble, sit, stand, amble, and stand some more. Blank-eyed, my brain chewing on the murders I witnessed. So grateful to be told what to do as the grief and horror I had seen penetrate my skin, takes root.

In a picture snapped by a reporter, my husband Peter and I are surrounded by fire engines, police cars, other witnesses, and yards of yellow tape. The picture shows me leaning into Peter, who had arrived at the scene moments before it was sealed, my head burrowed into his neck, the full weight of my terrified body begging him to make me feel safe again. I recall only my primal need for his warmth.

After the helicopters and ambulances carry away the injured, we spend five hours with about thirty other witnesses corralled by yellow tape and police officers waiting to be interviewed by the FBI. Penned into the parking lot outside of the Walgreens, saturated in shock, I do not notice the covered bodies twenty-five feet away in front of Safeway.

Gabe Zimmerman, a dear friend and former colleague, is one of those killed. It wasn't until weeks later that I realize Gabe's body is nearby during those terrible hours. I would spend months of talk therapy grieving the fact I did not go sit by Gabe's body. Why had I left him there? Why didn't I hold his hand, stroke his dark hair, let him know he was not alone?

Why couldn't I have wrested the gun from the lunatic before he shot and killed my friends?

Steeped in shock, we are a group of blank-eyed zombies who know, at some level, we will spend our remaining years processing, holding at bay, images of what bullets do to a human body.

My life is spared because I left my cell phone in my car. Seconds before the gunman opened fire, I dash to where I parked four slots from the front of Safeway to retrieve my phone. Although I had worked for Gabby, I'd come to the Safeway on a shopping errand to buy salad dressing, and was surprised to see my former colleagues. Ron Barber, district director for Gabby and my former boss, asked me if Peter, a journalist, was going to cover the event.

"I'm not sure, I'll call him," I tell Ron, digging into my purse for my cell phone, which wasn't there. I had left it in the car.

"I'll be right back," I tell him but chat a moment with Pam Simon,

Gabby's outreach coordinator. "I have to go call Peter," I say, turning toward my car.

Moments earlier, I congratulate Gabe on his recent engagement. He was my successor as Gabby's director of outreach, and I hug him and squeal: "I am so excited for you! When are you getting married?"

"Not for a year and a half," he laughs, waving his hand in front of his face. "We have plenty of time."

Two minutes later, Gabe is dead.

◉

The bullets shatter the bright blue light of a perfect January morning. Missing me by seconds. Injuring and killing my friends. Split seconds that freeze terrified intakes of breath inside of me.

My every sense yanks me deep inside my own body where I huddle near the still-point of my heart. When the bullets stop, I am sealed in a bubble of silence. Only silence. All silence. A profound hush despite the cacophony of sound in the wake of a mass shooting: moans, shouts, sirens, helicopters, hands beating on hearts to sustain life, last breaths gasped for and lost.

Life shifts in an instant from concrete and salad dressing to mystery and soul. Instinct pulls me back toward firing bullets to help my friends. As I stare down, a voice, my voice, neither male nor female, instinctive and innate, speaks. The same voice that urges me out of harm's way seconds before the bullets fire. The voice insists, when I run back in and stare down at my bloodied friends: *Do Not Look Left.*

I look straight down on Gabby and hear a person beside her say, "She has a pulse, she has a pulse." I know she is being helped; I know there is nothing I can do. I listen to my own inner voice and keep my gaze on Gabby. I look not a tiny bit to the left, which saves me from seeing Gabe dead, Ron and Pam bleeding on the cold sidewalk. Images that would have branded my brain, stayed with me forever. The voice is crystal clear. Emphatic. I obey.

In this holy space, which had moments earlier been a Safeway parking lot, I see, not with my eyes but with my heart, a holy space with souls rising from dead bodies. A holy place where we are all prayer, forced to bear witness to the only indisputable truth of human life: existence teeters, every second, on the precipice of death, one heartbeat away.

Humbled, I know I will never again unhear my soul voice or unsee with the eyes of my heart. Awed, I know my vision and voice provide absolute proof that ours is a spirit-filled existence. Heart-deep not sky-high. Organic. Body and source as one.

◉

It is pointless to ask why some lived while others died but a nine-year-old and thirty-year-old? Dead? I understand why some curse God, lose faith, abandon all hope. Pointless deaths pose the ultimate unanswerable question that throbs at the heart of mystery. *Why?*

I did not know nine-year-old Christina who died but thirty-year-old Gabe was my friend and former colleague. A good one. One of the best. Bright future, big heart, engaged to be married, a son who went every year on vacation with his mother. Not a saint, by any means, but full of life and intellect and public service.

Grief offers a range of coping options: denial, anger, bargaining, depression, escape, rage, despair. Grief loops and jags, stuns and devours. Again and again. From my experience, the only acceptance that comes with grief is that one's life has changed.

The funeral for Gabe is one week and one day after the shooting, in the courtyard of the Tucson Museum of Art, attended by hundreds, all of us shaded by large mesquite trees and soothed by the soft rush of palm fronds.

Grief clogs my every pore. Denial, anger, bargaining, and depression cannot cut through the layers of grief. And acceptance? Not happening. I am sealed in Saran wrap.

I hold Peter's arm with all I have as we make our way into the courtyard. A blur of people, none of whom I want to talk to, not an ounce of small talk in me.

We pause near a three-foot retaining wall just outside the museum doors where I survey the sea of grieving people bobbling on white folding chairs. A podium. A mic. A table set with pictures of Gabe. *Breathe*, I tell myself, but all I manage are shallow gulps. A deep breath is not to be had.

And then I spot her: Pam in a wheelchair surrounded by family. My former colleague and friend. The one I chatted with moments before she was shot. The one face down on the concrete. Dead, I knew she was dead, *what should I do, what can I do*? I had no idea how to help. Rigid. Blood puddled beneath her. My friend. Telling me about her son's wedding one minute and dead on the concrete the next.

I had learned a few hours after the shooting that Pam survived but seeing her, alive, sitting up, smiling, knocks the breath out of me. My knees buckle, drop me to the ground. Peter huddles with me on the cold, hard concrete, both of us hidden by the wall.

A few minutes later, able to walk, we find seats at the end of an aisle. I spot Ron, also in a wheelchair, across the courtyard. My need to talk to Ron is overpowering. I had sent a letter to him at the hospital thanking him for saving my life that he likely never received. I am driven by the need to let him know, and inch my way through the crowd to where he sits in his wheelchair, surrounded by family and friends. I gently tap his shoulder; he looks up at me.

"You saved my life," I blurt. "If you hadn't asked me to call Peter, I would have been shot."

Ron, fresh out of the hospital, smiles and squeezes my hand. I know he does not grasp what to me is the enormity of what I so desperately need to tell him. Pam later tells me she felt as if I had saved her life. Had we not been talking outside the Safeway columns, she told me, she would have been in the shooter's line of first fire.

Fate is nothing more than a pinball machine, pinging from one person to the next, fleeting seconds of bells and whistles where one life is spared while another life is ended.

I hug Ron gently, whisper my thanks, and make my way back to my seat to remember Gabe, who was tall with black hair, a ready grin, easy self-confidence, and a big heart. Intelligent, in love, engaged, engaging, the finest of public servants who loved to have fun and a cold bottle of beer, and cleaned out his email folders every single day.

We cry for him, all of us in our white folding chairs bobbling on the vast sea of pain. Silence, not solace, answers our many prayers. Our trek through grief will be long and painful.

◉

A bracelet of mountains encircles the Tucson Valley in the Sonoran Desert, which is native land for the mighty Saguaro cactus. My Southern California childhood gifted me a deep love for mountains, desert, and ocean. As a child, I delighted in the gifts of water, mountains, sand, and sky that hard-wired me to seek solace in nature. In the months after the shooting, the natural beauty of the Sonoran Desert delivers.

Sabino Canyon, sculpted out of Tucson's Santa Catalina Mountains by monsoon rains and melting snow, is a haven in the Coronado National Forest. Saguaro, mesquite, and prickly pear dot the canyon whose streams are fed with winter snow melt and summer monsoon rains that overflow Sabino's dams and streams. The lone road that cuts up through the center of the canyon became a favored destination for me after the shooting.

I often go alone in the months after the shooting, feeling safe along the road and happy for the mile-marker proof of tangible progress up a steep hill. Past the one-mile mark, a small path winds down to the stream which, when the water is high, flows all around a large flat rock. The dry, flat area is reachable by hip-hopping across several smaller rocks and one long leap to reach the middle.

The balm of rushing water and the whisper of cottonwood leaves in the breeze comfort me as I gaze at the Catalinas through the branches. I breathe deeply and release into the solid flat rock. The cottonwoods whisper their wisdom, remind me of our shared DNA, my true family of origin. I feel myself, once again, in the arms of my elm.

Words have always been my go-to but I know the trauma lodged inside my body hides in places beneath words. I have begun seeing a therapist, which is helping, but nature lends its hand, penetrating my body, opening me to the preverbal world of profound connection.

My grief has a mind of its own and rears its head with little warning. One day, after a late afternoon yoga class, I walk out into a gorgeous Tucson dusk and am surrounded by the first glimmers of spring: bright green leaves on the mesquite trees, yellow brittle bush blossoms, the first baby lizard. I gulp in the slanting light and, boom, Gabe springs full-blown into my consciousness. A Greek chorus plunges a dagger into my heart with words I hear clearly: "He will never see another spring."

On my trips to the grocery store, I avoid the covered breezeway in front of Safeway where the shooting took place, a sacred Ground

Zero chocked full of memory and pain. Even on days the temperature hits 112 degrees, I veer out into the parking lot, preferring blistering sun to triggered images and pain.

A few months after the shooting, I chat with the manager of the Safeway as I check out. She had been there that day and knew I had been too. We trade recollections, and she walks with me as I roll my cart out the door.

"Where was he?" I ask her. We had been talking about Gabe. I knew generally where he was when he was shot but not the exact spot.

"Do you really want to know?"

"I think so."

She points to a spot inside the cement column, not far from where Pam, Gabby, and Ron had fallen and where I stood seconds before the bullets. I thank her and push my cart toward my car, eager to escape. As I hurriedly unload my bags, a bottle of olive oil shatters on the hot pavement. I start crying and do something I never would have done in usual circumstances: I jump in my car and get the hell out of there.

Dear 19:06 Seconds,

Here's what I don't understand. After every mass shooting the country erupts with talk of arming teachers, more locks on doors, armed guards, more guns. Violence begets violence. Guns beget guns. Death begets more death. A true world without end with no amen in sight.

Mass shootings explode in split seconds of time. Mere instants when you are sitting in class, watching a movie, singing a hymn, dancing and sweating, or just showing up at Safeway on a Saturday morning when bullets upheave lives with terror and confusion.

Do you know how fast an instant really is? I scream my question at the television news after mass shootings when people claim they could have stopped it. Do you know the confusion that litters those few seconds? What is happening? Where am I? Are those bullets or thunder? A car backfire or deadly weapon? Your brain clogs and fogs and you shake your head, and only then do you dive for cover or try and help others but more than likely, the bullets have done what they came to do.

I sit some days staring at my cell phone, thumbing through Facebook pictures, googling CNN, and, again, hit the stopwatch function and watch 19:06 seconds zip by. The time it took at Safeway to kill six, wound thirteen, and terrorize a host of witnesses and loved ones.

Nineteen seconds and six milliseconds. I time my natural breath and manage five inhales and exhales. Five eye blinks. 19:06 seconds: the time span in which I ran back in as he kept shooting. Five inhales and exhales. Five slow blinks.

Dear split seconds, please wake them up. Simple math banishes delusions of heroic saviors. Let us all quit worshipping at the altar of guns and ammo and face the fact that gun-lust is the biggest turn-on of our culture. Murderous eroticism that slimes. Deadly climaxes that cannot be altered with thoughts and prayers.

A wedding. Love and laughter. Celebration of new life, hope, future. Three months after the shooting, my niece Jennifer, my brother David's daughter, gets married. The ceremony is held at Tivoli in Laguna Canyon, a few miles from the Pacific Ocean with an outside garden for the vows and an indoor space for dining and dancing.

The Jackson Five, my three brothers and sister, and I are together.

My brother Don flies in from Austin with his girlfriend, Cynthia. My older brother Dan and his wife Patricia and my sister Gayle and her husband Bill drive in from Surprise, Arizona. My heart is happy.

The afternoon before the wedding, Peter, Don, Cynthia, and I visit the Mission at San Juan Capistrano, one of our mother's favorite places. As kids, we visited each year on March 19, the day the swallows returned to the Mission to build their nests in the eaves, and it turned out, the same date Mom died. Mom loved those swallows.

"Do you know, kids," she told us every year, "the swallows return every year, same day, to build their mud-daubed nests?"

The Mission gardens feature cacti, Mexican Bird of Paradise, and roses. Mom packed a picnic lunch with bologna sandwiches and homemade chocolate chip cookies, food made more exotic when eaten away from home. Dad brought cold Cokes in a small ice chest, and we ate on a blanket spread beneath one of the sycamore trees.

Mom has been dead for thirty-three years when we gather for Jennifer's wedding, but her adoration of the Mission, a few miles from the hotel where we are staying for the wedding, lives on in us kids.

"Come on, Jack," Don urges me, using the nickname he has called me since childhood. I had wondered out loud if we have enough time before the wedding. "It won't take long and you know how much Mom loved it."

He is right. The afternoon is gorgeous, and we stroll, take pictures in front of the Mission, find swallow nests in the eaves. At one point, as Peter and I stand in line for information, I look across the grounds and see Don in front of one of the displays. My heart leaps. I miss my brother and am thrilled to share time in this special place. Over the years, with him in Austin and me in Washington, DC, we had not been able to see one another often enough. Peter takes a picture of Don and me in the gardens that day, both of us in sunglasses staring at the camera with our nearly matching smiles.

Don and I dance that night at the reception, fast and sweaty beneath glittery white lights, a kind of jitterbug as he twirls me in a circle, spins me in toward his body, and then unfurls me out and away. I wiggle in the air the index finger of my other hand just like Mom when she danced and giggled in our kitchen.

Happiness breaks through the grief in my body.

Later that night, Don and I walk together with our family through the darkened parking lot. "We are meeting for breakfast tomorrow," I remind him. "It's Palm Sunday."

"We have an early flight," he says. "Gotta get back to Austin." He and Cynthia are staying at a hotel a few miles from the hotel where the rest of us are, so I know there is no way to see them the next morning.

I squeeze his arm, snuggle my head against his shoulder. "We gotta do this again!" I tell him. "This has been too much fun! You and Cynthia need to come to Tucson."

"We will," he tells me. "Soon."

◉

Triggers. Everywhere triggers. A picture of Gabby in the newspaper, the backfire of a car, or a trip to the grocery store shatter my daily efforts to return to normalcy and rip open, again and again, my wounded innards by flashing me back to bullets and death.

Writing in my journal helps. Specific dates written before each entry cement me to the ground. I am alive. I saw this. The dates root events into careful slots where they stay and behave.

June 28, 2011

Gabby and Mark, a former astronaut and commander of the Space Station, attend a ceremony at the Space Center in Houston when Mark is awarded a Spaceflight Medal. Gabby, nearly bald, wears a beige scarf, light shirt, jeans, and sneakers. I watch the news clips showing her waving, smiling, and focused as she climbs the steps to board a plane. Gabby stares hard at the steps, as if willing her legs to walk. She takes the steps of the plane, one, two, three clear to the top. My heart leaps with joy to see her managing steps, and I replay the video again and again. I had not seen Gabby since the shooting and am hungry for information. Her image on camera shows her alive and mobile. She has risen.

July 5, 2011

I dream of Gabby. We are at a television station where she has organized interviews. She asks me to talk about the Tucson nonprofit I helped found and now head up. I am thrilled to see her and want desperately to hug her hard and long. But I don't want to be too emotional, so I hold back. She is like she always had been: sharp, clear, articulate. She limps but seems like her old self.

August 24, 2011

I dream I am dead. I have no idea how I died but am definitely dead. My body, covered in a sheet, lies on a twin-sized bed, and I stare down at it. I can see my foot and notice I had missed a few hairs on my left ankle when shaving. My ankle looks so vulnerable. I am not ready to be dead; I don't want to leave my sweet life of so much love and friendship, I think to myself that Christ got back into his body, so maybe I can too? I realize I have twenty-four hours to rest a bit until I have to get back into my body or be dead. I knew I hadn't decided to be buried or cremated but I wanted cremation—the alchemical fires.

The terror of the dead-dream shakes me awake. I head outside, take off my pajamas, and walk into our pool until I am neck-deep. The water restores me.

A bit later at our patio table with my journal and a cup of coffee, a Harris's Hawk flies above my head close on the heels of a finch. The breeze from the hawk's flapping wings brushes my cheek. The hawk swoops and misses, swerving away from the wrought iron gate as the finch escapes through the narrow slats and flies away.

Nature, raw and real. A milkweed bug crawls across my bare shoulder that I smash without thinking. Its dead body falls on the pages of my open journal.

⊙

My older brother Dan and his wife Patricia set up tables in the garden beside the pool. Dan roasts the turkey and makes Grandma's cornbread and biscuit dressing. Patricia, a master gardener, spins the yard into a wonderland of roses, mesquite, Mexican Bird of Paradise, bougainvillea, lantana, and desert lavender.

My family is good together at Thanksgiving. A favorite holiday for all of us. Don, in Austin with his kids, is the only one not there. We call them after dinner and pass the phone from one to another, struggling to hear over the din of family.

A week later, I call Don on my way to work, needing to hear his voice without the noisy background.

"We missed you last week."

"I wish we could have been there. It would have been a lot of airplane tickets."

"There was a moment," I tell him. "Peter and I were sitting on a bench at the side of the yard and looked across the yard at everyone around the tables. I love them all to pieces but they just don't get me like you do."

Don is the one I can talk philosophy, books, wellness, and family dynamics with. What does it all mean? We can ponder that one for hours and it doesn't much interest the others.

"I don't know what I'd do without you," I tell him.

"Me too," he says, "I love you, sis."

◉

Eleven days before Christmas, I sit at the island in our kitchen, a fresh cup of coffee in hand, enjoying a morning with no plans. Two days earlier, I had pulled off a major fundraising event for the nonprofit I headed. My board chair had just called to let me know I would receive a bonus check for the year. I was thrilled to have a few weeks off to celebrate the Christmas holidays. Talk therapy, nature, and time were luring me out of my cocoon of grief.

The first-anniversary commemoration of the shooting was planned at the University of Arizona on January 8, 2012. Gabby would be there. I had not seen her in person since I stared down at her on the Safeway sidewalk. I need a hug and am eager to reach the one-year mark and let go of constant memories of this-time-last-year.

My cell phone buzzes, and I can see it is Cynthia, Don's girl-friend, calling from Austin. *Why would she be calling?* I think as I hit the answer button.

"Don had a seizure," Cynthia blurts. "The hospital needs to know your family history."

"A seizure?" I search my brain. "Our aunt had to take seizure medicine," I tell her. "Is he okay?"

Don is an athletic, very fit chiropractor. He loves any sport that involves a ball, runs half-marathons, and inherited our mother's thin frame and constitution, which means he's never worried about weight gain. He is the last person among our siblings I imagine might face serious illness.

"We don't know much yet," Cynthia says, promising to call back. I call my sister and brothers in Surprise, AZ. Within a few hours, we will know about the inoperable cancer that forms a butterfly lesion across both lobes of his brain.

I frantically arrange our flight to Austin and search for a place for our dog to stay. When we arrive, Don is in a coma in the ICU, his lifeless hand wrapped around a small rubber ball one of his buddies has placed there, in case he wakes up and wants to shoot some hoops.

"Get up, goddamn it," I whisper in his ear. "You look fine."

The entire family shows up in Austin. The Jackson Five together one last time. The hospital staff, knowing Don's dire prognosis, allows as many members of our large family as can fit around his bed to stay as long as we want.

I have a few minutes alone with him.

I sit close to his head, clasping his hand, stroking his skin, a dark December sky outside the window of his room in ICU where his oxygen tank whirs, and bright lights flash his vital signs. The smell is antiseptic, not evergreen, but I sing "Silent Night." More whisper than song, my voice catches several times as I sing and release him.

He dies on December 21, slipping through the shifting light of the winter solstice without regaining consciousness.

A few days before Don's death, my sister Gayle has a dream in which Mom shows up in Don's hospital room, a bright glow in the corner, clear as can be.

"I've got him," she tells Gayle in the dream. "He's fine."

At this point, Don had been in a coma for two days. None of us have much hope he will recover, but we haven't given up either. When Gayle shares the dream with me, we both know he is not coming back. There is some comfort knowing Mom has snagged the child who was so much her same blood. She wants him back, and she took him.

"I think Mom saw him when we were in San Juan Capistrano and snatched him back," I tell Gayle.

The circumstances surrounding Mom's death were eerily similar to Don's. She died nearly the exact number of days into her fifty-eighth year as Don. She died of a brain tumor and was in a coma for eleven days before her death. Don died of a brain tumor that left him in a coma for seven days. Coincidence? Probably. But I draw comfort from the murky lines between life and death, verified by laws of physics, which prove time does not flow in linear fashion. No tidy demarcations of now and then amidst the blur, Mom yanked Don into her realm.

Two months before Don collapses, he sends an email to Gayle, David, and me asking if we remember the song from the 1950s, "Wringle Wrangle" by Fess Parker.

"Mom taught me all the words," Don writes. "Do you guys remember it? Did she teach you?"

I have a vague memory of the song's jingle-jangle lyrics but have no recall of Mom singing it to me but its main message is there is no need to cry about death when a pretty woman loves you.

"Mom never sang me that song," I joke to Don. "She always loved you best."

"Of course, she did," he replies. "Get over it!"

We know Don will soon die, but I take comfort in knowing Mother loves him and will welcome him back with all of her love. Don has a pretty woman's love.

◉

We fly back to Tucson from Austin on December 22 and return to a decorated Christmas tree with not one present beneath the branches. As a near Christmas baby, born on December 28, I marinate in all things Christmas. I host cookie-decorating parties, unpack bright red Christmas dinner plates, and hang ornaments dating to the 1970s, unwrapping each one slowly, deliberately, all of them sacred reminders of the friends who gave them to me or of trips we have taken. Peter and I spin our house into a concoction of evergreen, poinsettias, and candy canes.

Not this year.

Baking, shopping, and wrapping require too much energy. I sit for hours staring at the lights on the tree and the Santa Catalina Mountains outside our front window. On December 23, Peter and I drive to Tubac, an artist's village forty miles south of Tucson nestled among the Santa Rita and Tumacacori Mountains, twenty-three miles from the Mexican border. We agree to wander the town separately, find a few gifts for one another, and call Christmas done.

"I'll meet you in an hour at Tubac Jack's," Peter tells me, one of our favorite haunts in Tubac, an old-time mix of restaurant and saloon. I wander the shops with their million variations of Mexican metal sculpture, silver and turquoise jewelry, and fine arts. A turquoise glass cowboy hat catches my attention. The hat is about six inches brim-to-brim, suspended on a curved iron hook, hanging on a black leather strip. I buy it immediately, knowing it is more tribute to Don than gift for Peter, a variation on boots hung backward on a horse to honor a dead cowboy.

The hat sits to this day on our mantle, beside a picture of Don and me at the beach when I was thirteen and he was ten. I glare at the camera Dad holds because I have washed my hair and am not camera-ready. Don stands behind my left shoulder in madras shorts, white T-shirt, and goofy sun hat, beaming proudly behind his older sister.

Peter finds for me a glittery paper butterfly he clips to the edge of my Christmas stocking. I cry when I see it Christmas morning.

"Don," I tell Peter. "The butterfly lesion in his brain."

Three days after Christmas, on my birthday, we climb a ridge in Pima Canyon that juts over the Tucson valley. We sit on the hard ground, the valley spread out before us, and light a votive candle at the exact time Don's funeral service begins in Austin. A second memorial is set for January 8 at Del Rosa Methodist in San Bernardino, so we honor Don from a distance for this one.

Our candle flickers but stays lit against the breeze. My body molds to Peter's side as we sing "Silent Night," our hushed voices drifting through the soft desert light.

◉

I sit at a picnic table in the dog park at Brandi Fenton Park in Tucson two weeks after my brother's death. A woman I do not know sits next to me. We watch our dogs. Mid-morning and Zoe, our beagle, sniffs at the far wall. We chat. I am dressed in old sweats, my hair still bed-heady. I feel frumpy and shlumpy with grief. I don't care.

"There is a butterfly memorial in the park," she tells me. "Have you seen it? It's worth a visit."

Butterflies. The word cuts through me. *Shit*, I think to myself. Another trigger on my list: grocery stores, banks (often robbed by people with guns), the pop of fireworks, the fourth parking slot from the front of the Safeway, and now, butterflies.

"I haven't," I answer, images flitting through my brain of the killer butterfly lesion that killed Don. I jump up from my seat.

"Gotta get going," I tell her, too grief-soaked to worry about being impolite. I pick up Zoe, sweat pouring off me.

I know, absolutely, I will not visit the exhibit.

Three days later, Don's voice draws me into the nearly empty sanctuary of our family church, Del Rosa Methodist. His hometown memorial service lands on the same day as the one-year anniversary of the shooting. Doesn't get much better than that.

Where I need to be is with other survivors, hugging Gabby, crying together, marking the end of our this-time-last-year slog through 2011. Where I am is Del Rosa Methodist Church, the church I grew up in. A bank of windows to the north offers views of the San Bernardino Mountains and the wall behind the altar features nine stars, arranged like a large cross, each stained-glass pane depicting Jesus's life: in the manger, walking with a lamb, in front of a group of kids and, at the top, in his long white robes, Jesus raises his arms toward heaven.

He has risen. Don has died. I pray I will survive this day.

My brother's best friend, Geoff, greets me at the entrance to the church. He has created a CD of songs that Don had written and played on his guitars. Don's voice floats over my head as Geoff sound-tests before the service begins.

Geoff and I hug for a long moment as my brother's voice washes over us. I picture Don's tan fingers with their scattered tufts of black hair plucking each guitar string as he sings.

"I don't know if I can handle this but I love hearing his voice."

"Me too," Geoff agrees.

My heart clenches hard in my chest. Don was my baby brother. The one I proudly held in my just-shy-of-four-year-old lap in the back seat of our car as Dad drove us home from the hospital when Don and David were born. The one I gazed up at when he still swam with

David in my mother's belly. His death feels like the teeth marks of a wild animal who digs hard and leaves shattered flesh dangling from blood-spattered fangs.

Others begin to arrive, and I make my way toward the front of the church. My family and neighbors from our childhood fill the first two rows. The church is full to capacity, the one saving grace when someone dies young. I stand at the railing where I had stuck out my tongue at my first communion waiting for the body of Christ. The railing has a small plaque, still shiny after thirty-four years, etched with a tribute to Mom: *In Loving Memory of Madeline Jackson*. Dad had donated in honor of Mom's life and the church used the funds for a new railing, altar, and pulpits each with a plaque bearing her name.

Mom is everywhere.

Don's voice overhead sings a song he had written about growing up on Mountain Avenue, a few short blocks from the church: *They did their best with what they had, Shared their love with the kids too, a house of love and laughter, on Mountain Avenue.*

Mom, Dad, and Don are dead. The house has been sold. Our family of seven has shrunk to four. An image haunts me of all seven of us lost at sea. Four of us cling to small floats as we search for the faces of the other three who have slipped below the surface. Drowned. Gone. It takes all my energy to cling to the small float that bobbles me on roiling waters.

Images of Don in the hospital bed flood through me. He looks so damn healthy as if any minute he will quit joking, open his eyes, grab my hand, and say, "Let's get out of here, Jack." Did Don know he had a brain tumor? He had not mentioned any concern and, in fact, had run a 10K two weeks before he died. He should not be dead. Denial and anger joins forces inside of me.

Near the end of Don's service, I climb into the tall pulpit to speak on behalf of our family. The church is full of Don's friends and family. When Dad died in 1993, Don and I both offered eulogies to the congregation at Del Rosa Methodist, as we had done for our mother's death in 1978. Don and I were the public speakers in our family. Now I am alone.

"Don was the funny one," I begin in a halting voice. "Don was the daring one who rode his skateboard down the sheerest cement embankments and skimmed the highest waves in the Pacific on his surfboard. He wrote songs and sang them in public, alone with his guitar under a stage light. He always knew how to lighten me up."

I shift to a personal note, and share that it is the first anniversary of the shooting and that I had worked for Gabby and watched my friends shot and killed.

"Death can come out of nowhere," I tell them. "Live big every day, find an open mic and sing, tell jokes, hug often and sweat, every day sweat. Don's legacy. He will live in our hearts forever."

I climb down from the pulpit and make my way to the front pew, grasp Peter's hand and link my left arm with David, Don's fraternal twin. Geoff has produced a slideshow of pictures that ends with a video clip of Don on his back in the snow, big grin on his face, gliding his arms up and down, creating an angel in the snow.

Dear Self-Pity,

I have had enough. No, I have had more than my share. I love surprises as much as anyone but bullets and brain cancer eleven months apart? Witnessing the murder and wounding of my friends and then a dead brother? Uncle. Just, Uncle.

The truth is I am not a fan of self-pity. I am more of the what-can-I-learn-from-this school of thought, a believer in the "pick yourself up by your bootstraps and get back out there" messages from my parents. But I have my limits. I was just getting better after the shooting. Finding my way back into life, love, laughter. Did you have to drop another rock on me? Did I do something bad to deserve all this? And why Don? He was the healthy one. The funny one. The one who got me.

Why Don?

I realize "why" questions about death lead only to despair. I also know I am taking a day for self-pity. My sister Gayle calls them "pity parties." And yes, I need one. I might get a cake and crepe paper and light candles and blow them the fuck out, snuff out their light with the power of my breath. I might lie in bed all day, wallow in pain and resentment and then pop a bottle of champagne and raise a toast to poor, poor me.

Ok, this feels good. I promise not to stay here but it feels good. I am tired. I seem to be tired a lot. Anxiety and stress take a toll on my puny human body. They spit, pop, and jerk my nerves into frazzled frenzies.

A bubble bath, maybe, would ease my body, but I'm not in the mood. I need to sit here, do nothing, and feel sorry for myself. I want every ounce of my cortisol to stir me into resentment. I don't want any self-help New Agey inspirational claptrap to lure me out of this. I'm gonna roll in it, smear it all over me, liquify and drink it down, sauté a hot plate of pity and eat it for lunch.

Poor, poor me. I will open my heart back up when I am damn well ready.

◉

Hope is essential to unearthing a hiccup of joy in the midst of trauma, and joy is what is most needed when slogging through. For the first few months, I accept that joy is not to be had. I have no energy for defiance. *How can I open my heart when it's been shattered?* Bereft. Bleak. Leave me alone.

Several months in, a hopeful voice from within cuts through my belly, tases my heart: *Do not surrender to grief. If you do, the shooter and cancer have won.* I listen.

I begin to flirt with glimmers of joy: staring into night skies with slitted eyes that turn the sky into a silvery slivered light show. Zoe, our rescue beagle, jumps into my lap and nuzzles my cheek. The warmth of my husband's hand in mine as we watch the sun slip slowly behind the Catalina Mountains.

My rogue knows brokenness is the heartbeat of change, new choices. True rogue energy does not judge or shake you into action. Rogue never says, *get busy, get over it.* Rogues know grief takes time and travels a different path, winding, circling back in and out again. Rogue invites you into an imaginary womb, a saltwater haven that gentles the soul. *Take all the time you need,* Sweet Rogue whispers. *All the time you need.*

Rogue energy calms the cortisol spurting through me, knocks on my heart-door, and wiggles up and through the small details of everyday life. I wonder at the audacity of an ant carrying a crumb twice his size across the patio toward the small hole he calls home. A flickering candle flame and the fragrance of lavender offer calm. I delight in the upside-down when I am in a Downward Dog pose. The feel of sunshine on my just-shampooed hair. Peter's heartbeat when I rest my head on his chest. Flipping the pillow over to the cool side.

I swear I feel my DNA shift, loosen, and open a different path forward with each glimmer of joy. My life hits a hard stop as grief morphs me into a different me.

RECLAIMING BODY

The body never lies. What you say, you say in a body. You can say
nothing outside this body. You must awaken while in the body, for
everything exists in it: Resurrect in this life.

—The Gospel of Philip

A ROW OF TEN eucalyptus trees line Amy's street in Tucson, two blocks from the usually dry Rillito River. I arrive at my first appointment twenty minutes early and park beneath the towering trees. Google landed me on Amy's name, a national expert on treating depression with yoga and breathwork and, my luck, she lives in Tucson.

The day is gorgeous. I turn off the motor, open the car windows, and lean my head against the headrest. Grief, bed-rocked inside of me by the shooting, is now freshly layered with grief over Don. Breath is not easy.

Amy lives in a two-story condo with a sky-lit loft on the second floor. She has curly blond hair, somewhere in her fifties with a warm smile and first-hand experience with the ways in which yoga, sound, and breathwork unloose depression and anxiety from the body. She has written books about the effectiveness of yoga and breathwork that eased her own struggles with depression. Not a whiff of New Age wafts off her. I feel safe in her competent hands.

We sit in the loft space, sun flooding the skylights. I had emailed an intake form a few days earlier and shared what grief was doing to my body since my brother's death. I had gained seven pounds. My body feels leaden, as if all the brine has leaked out. I imagined yellow crime scene tape knotted around my throat, constricting my breath, my vital organs gasping for oxygen.

Amy's voice and petite frame belie her enormous spirit. She sits in a chair to my left and I sit in the middle of her couch. The sunshine sets her white-blond hair aglow. Maybe I was looking for an angel, but her countenance fills me with confidence.

"I am not a therapist," she reminds me when I describe my anxiety. The same words Olympia had used at Omega. Amy listens carefully and invites me to the yoga mat spread on the floor. On some days I arrive sluggish and depressed and on others I feel jumpy and irritated. She offers just the right postures and breathwork for whatever mood I bring with me.

We end each session with me in Child's pose, hips toward heels, my forehead on the mat. She sits behind me, her voice soft, both hands lightly touching my back, her voice soothing.

"Let it go," she urges. "You are safe," she says as she gently strokes my back, holding her hands still and then lightly brushing. Amy's touch triggers a memory of Mom's soft voice when she sat on the side of my bed on nights I could not sleep and stroked the space between my eyebrows with her thumb, reciting a poem I adored, "The Sugar-Plum Tree."

The eucalyptus trees outside Amy's apartment offer another source of comfort. *Come, sit, lean into me.* The trees are easily six feet in diameter, their whisper urgent. I have no desire to ignore their pull on me, and sit beneath them after every session with Amy. Fanny to the ground, I lean into the speckled bark, not caring if my clothes get dirty or if anyone can see me. The hard bump of their bark bites into my spine and skull. Birdsong floats down from high branches. Safe, I close my eyes and feel a sense of peace penetrate my body. A sensation I feared I would never know again.

◉

"Are you ok?" the yoga teacher asks as she quietly walks around the room watching us students find our way into Mountain pose, a standing posture where you root into place and sink into the grounded strength of mountain energy. I do as she instructs: feet planted parallel on the mat, a fist-width apart. I shrug my shoulders up and back to open my heart space. Fully rooted. All ten fingers atingle. Fully receptive.

I stand quiet. Fully focused on my breath. My tears roll silently down both cheeks.

"I'm okay," I whisper to the teacher. "I'm not used to standing still. Just breathing. It makes me sad. I'm always so busy."

"It's okay," she whispers back. "Yoga brings up lots of emotions. Pay attention and then release."

A sense of calm (all new, what was that?) settles in me. I fall in love. Yoga is a practice that does not run me hundreds of miles but instead invites me to root in place, breathe deeply into my own body, be present, quiet my monkey mind, and send giant gulps of breath and deep twists of blood to my belly and internal organs. *I'll have what she's having,* I think to myself as I look around the room and see women of all sizes on mats of all colors standing, just standing, quiet and calm.

Twist, cleanse, open, release, replenish, repeat.

A soul journey requires full-body exploration and buy-in. Yoga delivers. The practice engages my entire body as it limbers, loosens,

opens my heart, roots my feet, and opens new awareness, great possibility, in my DNA. You gotta feel rooted and safe if you want to dive
soul-deep. Mountain pose releases even more tears.

"Bring your whole heart to the mat," I am told again and again.
"Feel love and spirit flowing through you."

Yoga is my salvation. I fall deeply in love with yoga's imprint
on my body. Caressing, curving, bending, and squatting. The best
kind of lover who knows my body well and whose only interest is
in making me feel good. Yoga engages my creativity, stimulates my
imagination, strengthens my heart, tightens my core, tames my hormones and nerves. A masterful touch that unlooses fear from my
hips and thighs, breaks open my heart, and alerts my DNA to new
ways of living in the world.

Yoga has me at hello.

◉

A pair of mourning doves build a nest in the eaves of our patio. They
take turns sitting patiently on two eggs for two weeks until they hatch.
This morning, flurries in the nest. Mommy flies in, Daddy flies out
while the little ones puff out their wings, flap-flapping, and then sit
back down, Mommy huddling near them. They repeat this a number
of times but now, in the late afternoon, they remain in the nest. Not
quite ready to fly but flight is imminent.

You died, dear Mother, before I was ready to take flight. You were
there and then vanished, leaving me all alone in the twigs and sticks of
the shaky life I had built. I know I was old enough to fly on my own. The
sheer chronology of twenty-eight years on Earth should have grown
me wings on which I could soar. But my heart was too shaken by my
divorce, my body run amok with passion. I was unmoored, untethered,
and not yet trusting my own strength, intelligence, or talents.

Here is the truth: You have morphed from flesh-and-blood Mother to Mother-Spirit who remains alive and well inside of me today. I long to sit with you in person, two cups of coffee in front of us. You could even smoke a cigarette because, hey, you are already dead. We would talk, woman to woman, share the pain in our hearts and the joy in our bellies and how upset you were with me when I left Jim. You would speak the truth about your relationship with Dad and how difficult it was to birth and raise five children.

Do you realize we never had an adult conversation, truthful and heartfelt, peer to peer, you and me? I long for just one. Honest and true. The question I long to ask you: Are you proud of the woman I have become?

You would love Peter. He has a big heart and good values and a nice little ass and a quietness and love of nature much like you had. It took me many years on my shaky wings to build a nest with him. But we did, and we are still here thirty-four years later.

I am grateful your spirit remains so alive within me. I learned to fly, Mother-Spirit, and feel you always at my back, your love keeping me aloft. Turns out, I had you long enough for me to make it in this world. Turns out your passion for virginity, which I tried so hard to maintain for my first twenty years, transformed to a passionate soul I claim as my own. My fuel-source and fire.

◉

"No," I tell Kathy, my fellow classmate in yoga teacher training. "I cannot do that. No, just no. I'm not gonna even try." My words. My fear.

Forward folds are easy for me. Both palms flat on the floor, piece of cake. My nose easily touches each knee when I stand or sit. Move forward, bend forward, I am all about motion that takes me ahead.

Flexes me into the future, I've got this, I'll try harder. I know I can do it better, longer. Forever bending and striving for perfection.

Backward? Not so much. I don't want to go back there, regret doesn't do much for me. What's the point? My motto: Look to the future, flex it forward. Let's get this done.

Yoga is not buying my life philosophy. I am training to be a yoga teacher and I do not have the option to offer an entire class of forward folds. The mighty backbend lurks, taunts, and dares. And the mightiest backbend of all, Heroine's pose, stands ready to call my bluff.

I know the pose is generally known as Hero's pose, but, for obvious reasons, I choose Heroine. The pose becomes my holy grail of yoga teacher training.

For months, I gently ease my shoulders backward, both hands supporting my lower back, but never make it to the ground. When I am on my belly, I can reach behind me, grab both feet and ease myself into Wheel pose with both knees bent, my arms close to my side as I grab hold behind me of each foot keeping pelvis planted on the mat.

Camel pose? I can do that one too. Me on my knees, hands up over my head, and then arching my back as I move one hand to each heel. Camel pose cracks open my heart. I feel vulnerable and receptive. Maybe I can avoid Heroine's pose and stick to Camel and Wheel? Both are backward bends. Isn't that enough? Maybe I don't have to try for the holy grail. Who needs a heroine anyway?

But then comes that day. We are nearing the end of months of training, and I am relieved Heroine's pose has not shown its face. Maybe they will forget to teach us that pose? Maybe I can escape unscathed?

Sue is our teacher that day, a yoga instructor and registered nurse with extensive expertise in anatomy and physiology. I trust her completely. But that morning, as I sit on my mat, Sue announces that Heroine's pose, as if it were nothing, is next up for us to learn.

I freeze on my mat. Maybe I can go into the bathroom and not come out. Maybe I can claim a stomachache and leave all together. "Find a partner," Sue tells us. "Hero's pose is my favorite."

Kathy sits on the mat next to me. She and I have become friends, and we do the let's-partner wink and nod to one another.

"I can't do this," I say to Kathy. "I don't even want to try."

"You can," she encourages me. "We need some props."

Heroine's pose is a seated yoga posture that stretches the quads. Hips are on the mat with both legs bent at the knees, feet point backward on either side of the body. Many little kids sit with ease in the pose every day, their hips and legs forming a perfect "W" shape on the floor. I can kneel and do squats but forcing my butt to the floor between both legs has never worked for me even as a child.

Sue explains the posture and instructs that once our bodies are in a perfect W shape with hips on the mat, all we need to do is ease the back of our heads to the floor. I have no idea why they would call this pose Hero's or Heroine's—on your back, knees bent, head to the mat and heart open is as vulnerable as you could get. Maybe, just maybe, the pose is saying that making yourself vulnerable is the strongest thing you can do? I am not interested in metaphors as I search for excuses so Kathy will not make me do the pose.

"I am a runner," I beg, "I have strong quads that don't like this deep stretch."

Kathy ignores me. By this time, I am seated on my mat, knees bent, my butt not reaching the floor. She places a bolster beneath me. *Ok, ok, maybe*, I think to myself as my hips reach the bolster, settle in.

"Good work," Kathy encourages. "Look at that. You are nearly there. All you have to do is lean backward toward the floor."

"No way."

She piles a second bolster behind my back. If I can't bend backward enough to reach the floor, she will bring the floor to me.

"Try again," she urges. "You got this." She keeps her left hand on my right shoulder; her voice is low and comforting, but she is not letting me off the hook.

I slowly ease back, trying to find the bolster behind me.

"Keep going," she urges. "You're nearly there."

I am sweating, my thighs screaming while my heart urges me back and down. A few more inches and . . . contact. My legs still extend by my sides with feet pointed behind me in a perfect "W." The eagle has landed! I have arrived on the Moon's surface, a large step for womankind. Heroine courage and pride surge through me.

"I did it!" I smile up at Kathy, quickly correcting myself, "I mean we did it."

"You did it." She smiles back at me.

I lay there feeling proud but also deeply vulnerable. Lying on the ground, legs angled behind me forms a perfect "fuck me" posture, with heart open, knees wide apart. Heroine's pose is not finished with me. Here's the truth about yoga: Stretch and twist your body in ways you haven't been able to and you can release old stories, emotions you no longer need or are tired of holding. You will, if you pay attention, be gifted healing dreams.

My wide-open, heroine-cleansed hips gift me two big dreams:

The first night, I dream of Mom and me diving off a dock in perfect symmetry. Like synchronized swimmers, we hit the glass-smooth water and swim toward shore barely rippling the water. Side-by-side, our skin glistening, in unison.

The next night, I am kidnapped by a car full of men. Seven of us (same size as my family of origin) wedge into a car. They drive me to a house stocked with foods that are colorless, bland: clear chicken broth with white meat, white rice, oatmeal. Unflavored, stripped of fragrance and color, I am trapped in an all-male space, physically safe but devoid of texture, color, or taste.

I awaken from the dream with a giant aha. I worked for years in all male environments, bleached of color and with tamped-down emotions. I heard many times: *You feel too much. You worry too much. You care too much.* The dream reminds me of the communion wafer at my first communion, so long ago, white, flavorless, and stuck to my tongue. My bland initiation into the masculine worlds of churches and corporations.

I realize my rogue and my heroine are one and the same. I am the heroine of my own life, no red cape or magic bracelet required. Heroine's pose opens my body, unleashes my imagination, and paints dreams of clarity. I marvel at the sensation of being "just right."

Dear Weightlessness,

Did I tell you about the time I was at a business meeting at a woman's home just outside of Boston? A colleague and potential business partner, we meet with three others to explore what we might do together. A long morning, too much coffee, huddled round her dining room table, breaking for a stretch and bathroom break before lunch.

That's when it happens. I wander with two other women into the backyard and behold a wonder of wonders. A trampoline. Not just any trampoline. Not one that sits round and squat on shaky metal legs. This one is built into the ground in a space that had once been a swimming pool. A large rectangular in-ground pool but, now, instead of water sparkling its surface, taut, tight trampoline skin stretches end-to-end.

"May I?" I ask the woman, my colleague, to whom the trampoline belongs. "May I please?" I implore. The pull of that trampoline squashes any sense of business propriety, appropriateness, and good behavior. I need me a jump.

"Go for it," she invites.

I yank off my heels, glad I wore pants to this meeting and not a big fluffy dress, which, on second thought, could have made it even more fun ballooning up and down with the skirt flouncing and dancing with me. But pants will certainly do.

Her backyard is large with a house or two in the distance. Open vistas of green mountains glisten in the October light. I walk out across the vast surface of that Olympic-size trampoline, my feet trying to get their bearing, I lilt side to side until I reach the center where I steady myself and begin to bounce.

Small at first, little jump up and right back down but building momentum. Up and down, up and free, up and my heart sings, up and up, again and again. I spread my arms wide, let laughter and joy spill out of me. Freed of the bonds of earth and meetings and memos and conference tables and saying it right.

I am weightless, unbound by space and time, my heart hard-pumping great gulps of joy.

I swear this is my last yoga example but I must rave about the yoga pose known as Wild Thing. There absolutely should be a Rogue pose in yoga but Wild Thing comes darned close. Give it a try.

I am the sole student who shows up for a 5:15 p.m. heart flow yoga class taught by Chadwick at a downtown Tucson yoga studio. Chadwick is in his late thirties with dirty blond hair and a build that is more athletic than yogini. I have never had an individual yoga session, and my immediate inclination is to shrink into a bout of self-consciousness. Had I applied enough deodorant, would my yoga pants creep down or bunch up, and how many times had I worn this top and did it truly pass the sniff test?

We begin with three ohms—those juicy sounds that knit together body, voice, and spirit into a vibrating haiku of connection. With my first ohm, any shred of self-consciousness vanishes into the universe. The ohms vibrate through my throat and belly, and from the island of my yoga mat, I simply let go and join the adventure as Chadwick corrects, pushes, and prods, inviting me to go deeper.

The hour passes quickly and hits its crescendo with Wild Thing, a posture that requires an insouciant journey from Three-Legged Dog to tipped over that always makes me want to break into song. Chadwick urges me to arch higher, tilt further, stretch deeper. He stands behind, supporting the posture, and I lean and stretch deeper than ever before.

"I would fall over if you weren't backing me."

"Let's see," he replies, slowly stepping away from my arched, sloping body.

I stay in the posture sweating, aching in new places but also proud of my new "limit" that breaks open the ancient, hungry, and curious wild thing at my core. My rogue, alive and fully present.

After class, I walk out into a beautiful Tucson evening to meet Peter at Hotel Congress. My cheeks are aglow and sweat glistens my forehead. My hair is pulled back into a shabby little ponytail but I don't care. Inside of me, movement and breath simmer through my blood, bone, and marrow. I am springier of step, smiling, and, yes, a bit smug. A yogic orgasm.

My dream that night is of the divine feminine. Rita, the friend who had thrown those fortune-telling sticks for me when I first moved to

Tucson, shows up in my dream vividly present. The irises of her eyes are mandalas, geometric shapes that symbolize wholeness, fashioned in deep greens and bright blues with slashes of red and topaz.

Each time Rita shifts her head a fraction, the design in each eye morphs into a different shape, like a kaleidoscope, forever turning, creating new artistic renderings of wholeness. I stare deep into her eyes, in awe of the depth of beauty. Wild Thing opens my body to new adventure, crashes me through perceived limits, and gifts me kaleidoscopic images born of my anatomy and physiology. Rogue tumbles me through ever-shifting beauty and mystery.

◉

Peter comes into the kitchen where I am making dinner. His blue eyes sparkle and I know something's up. "Come outside a minute," he urges, extending his hand toward me. I put down the wooden spoon, turn off the burner, and take his hand. He leads me into our backyard where he has spread a comforter on the small patch of grass beneath the Queen Anne palms.

The late afternoon Sun has gentled its way west, and we gentle our way toward the comforter, wiggling out of shorts and shirts, loving the sensation of slanting sun on our bare bodies.

"It was just too pretty out here to stay inside," he says to me before our lips find each other and latch on.

My memory of our first kiss will never go away. We were sitting on the couch in my apartment in Arlington, VA, back from our first date to see Paul Newman in *The Verdict*. Seated side-by-side, fully clothed, he turned toward me and leaned in. I was thirty-three years old and had kissed many. But I shall never forget the feeling that floods my body when our lips touch.

I'm home, I say to myself. *Home*.

I know with every fiber of my being I am meant to kiss these lips for many more years. That does not mean it will not take much time and many battles to solidify our relationship. Both of us had been married before and carried with us over-stuffed baggage that had to be sorted, cleaned up, and discarded. But the memory of that first kiss always brings me home to Peter the several times we broke up, moved apart, and then tried again. The "I'm home," that floods my body with our first kiss convinces me, every time, to persevere through our struggles to land, again and again, home.

Our lovemaking on the comforter that afternoon, many years into our marriage, is not bodice-ripping release. Lovemaking morphs in relationships that endure for years. Slower, gentler, deeper. Our bodies know each other well. Our cogs and grooves are well-oiled and well-meshed. In my years of screwing around, I had hungered for what I found with Peter: a safe place where my passion is welcome and my broken heart opens wide.

"I love you," I whisper to Peter as we lay sweaty and satisfied.

"I love you too."

◉

My life has offered more experience with death than I had hoped for but death's guiding hand makes me smarter. I gotta take credit for stirring up my own DNA with yoga, breathwork, and sweat, but the truth is that death speeds up the process of change by stirring the root and blossom of my soul.

Death changes my worldview and focuses me on what means most in life. We all die, every single one of us, no matter what and, if we pay attention, death is the most transformative teacher of all. Inside-out transformation, tissue deep, gene-deep, enduring. Death lands us squarely within the heart of divine mystery.

What does death teach me? Mom's death leads me to Anne, who deepens my knowledge of dreams. Dad's diagnosis of lung cancer and imminent death inspires me to sign up with Olympia Dukakis, who teaches me prayers of sound and sweat, and guides me to feel, body-deep, my own power of Inanna. Witnessing the injury and death of my friends affirms divine spirit-voice inside of my heart. Don's death leads me to Amy and the healing power of breath, yoga, and touch.

Death is the ultimate shape-shifter of human lives. Olympia's advice about tears applies perfectly to lessons of dying: Get in your boat and row.

◉

Quit job, check.

Sell house, check.

Buy smaller house in Tucson, check.

Earn yoga teacher certification, check.

Get a new dog, check.

Two weeks into 2014, I shift into action, give my notice at the nonprofit I had helped found and where I had served as executive director since 2008. Raring to go, my *shibboleth* dream rears its head once again inside of me. Enough slog.

Soon after, Don shows up alive and well in a dream.

"Don," I shout and fall into his arms. "I am so glad to see you."

We hug. My heart soars.

"Why did you have to die?" I ask him.

Don begins to return to ether.

"Never mind, never mind," I cry. "We are all okay—it is okay you died."

My words bring him back, and I hold on tight, breathing in his spirit.

☉

Pitch black at 5:18 a.m. The last day of January 2018 and the Tucson sky is darkened by a total eclipse of the moon. I sit on a rock in our front yard, coffee in hand, watching the show. The moon did not totally disappear but pulses with orange light. By 6:15 a.m., the moon is fully shrouded. Peter comes out for a few minutes to watch.

The moon remains in darkness for nearly an hour, the curvature of its surface pulsing orange inside its belly. Our world adores transcendence: someone get me out of here. We pray and meditate to transcend, move out of our bodies, take us up and away. Immanence pulls us inside to a pulsing wisdom that knows intimately our profound connection with all of nature.

The eclipse offers visual proof of the immanence of moon, earth, and sun. In perfect alignment for a brief time, sun on one side, moon on the other, and earth splat in the middle. The moon holds the earth's shadow fat across its center, and I can nearly hear its orange throb. A line from a Pablo Neruda poem comes calling: *Under your skin the moon is alive.*

DEFIANCE

The defiance of established authority, religious and secular, social and political, as a world-wide phenomenon, may well one day be accounted the outstanding event of the last decade.

—Hannah Arendt

A WARNING: my thoughts on "defiance," the lifeblood of rogue, are offered as lecture. The Uffizi eyes lectured me and I, in turn, feel the need to parse their demanding eyes into words that are bossy and insistent.

As a psychotherapist, I know the power of story. I have benefited personally, and witnessed in others, the healing that comes from unearthing childhood stories of trauma and pain. I know the difficulty of naming our pain when it is inflicted by someone we love. I know the critical role of feeling and talking about one's pain *especially when it is inflicted by someone we love.* Our hearts long to share what hurts and to have it heard.

Speaking truth about what went on in our families of origin is tough work but it is not betrayal. Epigenetically, it is an essential step toward stopping the march of trauma through generations. A courageous act taken on behalf of our family lineage that can shift our present and future from pain and anxiety to health and well-being.

Ancestral trauma is no different than familial trauma. Both are inherited and huddle in our bodies, stifle our hearts, and lead us to unhealthy coping behaviors. My panic attack in the Uffizi convinces me both ancient and familial trauma are not subject to time restrictions. Shape-shifting through history is demanded.

Releasing ancestral trauma requires the same truth-telling, diving deep into lies we have been told—*you carry sin in your body; female sexuality and passion must be controlled.* It is essential to dissect these ancient stories and lies, and release the havoc they inflict. Be warned that with ancestral trauma, you are not just taking on your family of origin, you are taking on origin stories, ancient and embedded in our DNA, rooted in laws, creeds, and dogma that have held females hostage for centuries.

The biggest kahuna: organized religion. Our right to criticize or petition our government is protected by the First Amendment. Taking on the church is a whole other story. Memories of heresy, witch-burning, banishment, and confessionals are preserved in our DNA. Strap up. It's not an easy ride.

My search for truth takes me deep into ancient stories I was never taught in church or school. I must confront the lies I was taught in church and school. So many layers of story written to cement hierarchy and patriarchy in place.

Religion drove its fangs directly into male and female flesh when it joined forces with political leaders who were hell-bent on control and conquer. Religious dogma and creeds deified masculinity and glorified the penis while it deadened and outlawed female sexuality and divinity. A body-grab of breathtaking proportions begun in the earliest years of the Current Era that endures today.

My epigenetic trek through history lands me squarely in the time of Constantine who served as Roman emperor from AD 306 to 337, the first emperor to convert to Christianity. He masterfully *and expansively* extended and solidified the power and reach of his Roman Empire by joining forces with church leaders. He did not invent empire building but he expanded it into an artform.

Why should we care about any of this? Because if we do not know the truth of ancient stories, we will never be able to free our bodies from inherited trauma. Just like familial trauma, dredging up stories and understanding their impact on our bodies and reconnecting with emotions are required medicines to be taken regularly: *Remember, feel, release, claim.*

You are taking on big issues: Who invented sin? Why were women denied ranking in the church? Who determined wives were chattel? What is female sexuality without the narrowing of virgin-whore?

Ancient erasure echoes through our bodies today. Learn the truth, feel it body-deep, and free yourself from historical prisons. This lecture is done. Amen.

◉

A mid-December morning. Bright sun streams off the Catalina Mountains and sets aglow the glass créche that sits on our coffee table. Brightly lit, Joseph gazes down at his newborn son, his hand gently resting on Mary's back while two cherubs kneel, working double-duty as candle holders, hands in prayer, on either side of Jesus in the manger. The brightly lit créche stirs memories of my childhood belief in mystery and wonder larger than everyday life.

I saw the musical *Jesus Christ Superstar* a week earlier and cringe at Jesus's horrific death. A gruesome finale to his life on Earth that awaits him on that cold night he was born when there is no room in the inn, his baby flesh goose-bumped by frigid night air as he latches on to Mary's nipple and sucks life into his tiny frame.

As a child, I accepted all I was taught about God and Jesus but also fully accepted the connection with nature and mystery my elm tree assured me was mine. Grape juice and hard pews left me wondering but I believed in God. Period. In my twenties, I turned away from the church's judgment of my passion and nonvirginal body, and found God in nature.

Religion's impenetrable walls obstruct those who question or hunger for a different way through. My rogue makes me face this most formidable fortress and ask tough questions about organized religion. I need every defiant gene I have to persevere.

◉

The gift of Zoom, born of the pandemic, ushers a range of biblical scholars into my home to guide my search for religious truth. The pandemic also serves up ample time for research. I dive in. My Uffizi panic attack will not happen for several years, but I realize today my search for religious truth, begun in the early days of the pandemic, shifts my own DNA to notice and trust my mystical experience in the Uffizi when my electrified body tells truths I am ready to hear.

My dive into ancient history serves up proof of how tough it is to walk this Earth strapped in a female body. Olympia's instruction again kicks into gear for me. I need not only to *research* ancient stories but to *feel* how new truths resonate through heart, belly, and crotch.

The fearless Rogue who drops into my life courtesy of Zoom is Meggan Watterson, who feeds me full of new truths that nudge me into a whole new relationship with my body. She invites me to dig deeply into my own body and know I can heal my own brokenness if I claim respect and divinity and release shame and guilt.

Meggan, a theologian who earned master's degrees in theological studies and divinity from Harvard University and from Union Theological Seminary in New York, has written books that breathe life into ancient stories and details their relevance to female lives today.

Meggan's Zoom sessions unfold the Gospels of Mary Magdalene, Philip, and Thomas, none of which is included in today's Bible. She recommends *A New New Testament,* edited with commentary by Hal Taussig, who was Meggan's professor at the Union Theological Seminary. *A New New Testament* gathers in a single volume many of the Gospels and stories excluded from the Bible because they did not conform to the canon and creed of hierarchy. My copy is dog-eared.

Meggan characterizes Christianity during the first several hundred years after Christ as "a radical movement, an experiment that is still being formed and informed today." Mary Magdalene, Philip, and Thomas are among the "radicals" wandering and teaching of a Jesus and God as The Good inside every human. Their teachings run smack up against leaders of the Roman Empire and church who are hard at work empire building: conquering, murdering, and enslaving in the name of what would become known as the *Holy* Roman Empire.

In and around 325 AD, the thirst for taming or eliminating radical tribes intensifies. A group of bishops, at the behest of Emperor Constantine, all men of the higher classes, convene at the Council of Nicea to wrestle into a single church-body the disparate and radical tribes that flourish after Christ is crucified. The educated men understand the power of words to exert control. Write it down. Make it law, creed, and canon. And so they do.

The result: the Nicene Creed, written in 325 AD, flows out of them and onto papyrus. A creed still recited today: *We believe in one God, the Father almighty, maker of heaven and earth, of all that is seen and unseen.*

The one God in the Nicene Creed is Caeser's guy, and He and the emperor join forces to cement in place the hierarchical and patri-archal ethos of the Roman Empire. They construct hierarchies atop the bodies and souls of humans, and the Nicene Creed steamrolls in place the church-state partnership that leaves radicals as roadkill in its wake. The Bible is The Book and all other Gospels written by "radicals" are ordered destroyed.

Hats off to the radical monks who refused to destroy but instead bury the errant Gospels. Fifty-two of these "radical" Gospels were unearthed in Nag Hammadi, Egypt, in 1945, including poems, myths, and parables that depict Jesus and his teachings very differently than the books in the Bible. The monks showed true courage by hiding the texts, and their acts of bravery preserve today Gospels like Thomas and Philip.

Mary Magdalene's Gospel, unearthed in 1896, is lumped with the Nag Hammadi texts and all are labeled Gnostic Gospels, a term that can imply illegitimacy. In fact, Gnostic or gnosis translates as the "wisdom we acquire through direct experience." Direct experience. That which we feel and know to be true in our human bodies. Goose bumps and tears. The jolt of a stunning sunset. Knowledge born of direct experience is an area where females excel.

The defiance of monks who hid instead of destroying banned Gospels inspires me. A fresh and inspiring religious message that flows directly from our collective DNA.

Defiance is as much our birthright as erasure.

◉

In one of my last jobs in Washington, DC, I work for an especially beastly man. My first week on the job, a high-level lobbyist gig, my new boss walks past me in the hall several times without a welcome or hello. *Okay, that's how he wants it,* I think to myself. He had built the firm with his brother, two mover-shakers in the city. With staff, he is rude and cruel and obviously screwing around with one of the interns.

The last straw for me is the day a group of us meet in his office that has a glass door. His secretary has a question for him and starts through the open door. He quickly slams it in her stunned face, which can be seen through the glass. His disrespect for staff is widely known. In a profile of him in a respected political magazine, the writer asks him about his reputation. His response: "They aren't jumping out of windows, are they?"

I last four months. On one of the toughest days, I discover near our office building at 10th and G Streets in downtown Washington, DC, a Catholic church with an unlocked front door I slowly push open. There are a few people inside the dark sanctuary, so I slide into a back pew to soak in the cool and calm.

As my eyes adjust to the dim light, I look to my left and see a large statue of Mary. No baby in sight. Mary is carved out of pink marble and sits in a throne-like chair. My heart stops. I have never in my life seen a graven image of Mary as strong and powerful, by herself, no husband or baby in sight. Del Rosa Methodist offered very few female images. We had Mary, head covered as she gazes down at baby Jesus. That was it. Not a whisper of female divinity existing outside of any relationship.

In this Catholic church on a sultry, hot afternoon, I see her enthroned—large and pink and formidable. My blood races. A graven image of female divinity detached from motherhood. I see therefore I am. Her graven image stirs my imagination, excites my body. Divinity, pink Mary assures me, is mine to claim. The same message Meggan will teach me, years later, is written in banned Gospels.

What happened to pink Mary? Before the written word, oral traditions morph and nourish generations with tales of powerful female goddesses, nonvirginal and robust. The "female" divine that appears in the Gospels that didn't make it into the Bible.

The transition from oral to written did not happen overnight, but stories that had been shared over generations, sprung from hearts, marinated by tongues, and shot through with mystery and wonder are banned. Stories that celebrate the Sun that rises each day, the monthly dance of the Moon in female bodies, and the miracle of food sprouted from dirt, sun, and water are stripped of depth and connection with nature, embalmed on clay tablets and papyrus sheets.

Written words are locked into decrees, dogma, rules, mandates, and laws that dictate right and wrong, sin and evil, good and bad that bifurcate human lives. The world splits into "haves" who are educated and literate, and have-nots who are illiterate.

Sacred stories, not included in today's Bible but which survived, tell of connection, not conquer. Stories of Jesus and God who love all humans and give nary a whit nor a shit about sexuality. Pink Mary radiates female divinity and shimmers my DNA. With each breath, we are all fully human and fully divine.

Period.

◉

Gazing into the vast Sonoran sky cracks my heart open. When we first move to Arizona, farther from the ocean than I had ever lived, Peter is the first to say, "I don't miss the ocean because the sky is so huge." He is right.

When I gaze sky-high, I see divine spirit in the sky's brilliance of color and light displayed artistically every single day on nature's ever-changing canvas. The vast sky lavishes sunlight, moonlight, and stars.

Our backyard opens to gorgeous views of the Catalina Mountains. Every morning and evening, a rainbow of light washes across the face of the peaks blending from yellow to pink to blue. We face due east so we can watch the sun peek over the mountains each morning, and then behold the reflections across the full face of the mountains at sunset. And clouds: wispy to bulbous, soft pillows of white morph into spines and fish. I marvel at the deft hand of nature and soak its creativity into my every cell.

◉

Mary Beth, her husband Dan, and I meet monthly to read and discuss James Joyce's *Ulysses,* published in 1920. Dan, who taught the book as an English teacher, guides our way. We labor for a full year to parse the dense, long-sentenced, unpunctuated, and hallucinatory text as the hero Leopold Bloom stumbles his way around Dublin on a single day in June. The book ends with Molly Bloom's orgasm that is yes, all that, oh yes.

Joyce modeled the Molly character in *Ulysses* after Penelope, the woman at the heart of Homer's *Odyssey.* Penelope remains chaste, despite many suitors, awaiting her husband's return while Odysseus shares himself, liberally and with abandon, with an array of women.

Just saying.

Stories of female purity and male conquer run rampant through literature, but Joyce dives deeply into his vision of female orgasm with Molly's monologue in the last chapter. We do not know if Penelope was gifted a gigantic orgasm by her husband Odysseus when he finally makes it home from the Trojan War, but Joyce writes Molly's orgasm as the climax of *Ulysses*:

I was a Flower of the mountain yes when I put the rose in my hair like the Andalusian girls used or shall I wear a red yes and how he kissed me under the Moorish Wall and I thought well as well him as another and then I asked him with my eyes to ask again yes and then he asked me would I yes to say yes my mountain flower and first I put my arms around him yes and drew him down to me so he could feel my breasts all perfume yes and his heart was going like mad and yes I said yes I will Yes.

My beef with Joyce is that "yes." Much has been written about whether or not Joyce captured the rush and energy of female orgasm. He got the rhythm, yes, I say yes, he certainly did. But, in a 1921 letter, Joyce described "yes" as "the female word," which he interpreted as "acquiescence, self-abandon, relaxation, the end of all resistance." A female word?

Did Molly self-abandon or self-claim? My discovery of clitoral orgasm in my early twenties gifted me agency. All mine. Self-assuring. Self-claiming. I gave myself over to myself with a mighty Yes. I like to think Molly felt the same way.

I do not want my Yes written by one more male author, ancient or contemporary. No, I say, no, you do not know my Yes. My imagination unclogs as I name and claim divine spirit inside of me. My body assures me divinity is mine just as my orgasm is mine. My yes. My experience of divine power. Agency not acquiescence.

Write your own damn orgasm.

◉

Want to stand tall in the truth of your felt experience? Position yourself at the top of your yoga mat, place both hands on your hips.

Step your right foot halfway back on your mat, and ground through your heel and pinky toe. Bend your left leg and extend your left arm straight in front of you and your right arm in a direct line behind you.

The pose is Warrior II, but do not stop there. Gently move both arms and clasp your fingers together behind your back. Rest your hands on your lower back or a few inches off your back. Bow forward, head toward the mat as you hang inside your bent left leg.

Humble Warrior.

Feel blood rush to your brain. Open and close your jaw—loosen and release. Feel yourself bowing and fully humbled. Know with this bend forward you are turning on your parasympathetic nerves—your "off" button, the source of rest and digest.

Humility is unappreciated and underused. It is not weakness but is profound appreciation for our brief time on this planet. It is respect for all living things. Bow in humble praise to the natural world. Our world desperately needs individuals who hunger for humble. Hang a few moments, and then slowly unclasp your hands, extend them long in Airplane, and slowly rise to standing. Tune into the sensations in your body. Feel your connection with all that lives. Root into your truth.

◉

If you question the immense intractability of religion in our culture and world, whether you are a churchgoer or not, try writing about God. My friends ask me why I'm reading all this Bible stuff. *I need to know full truths,* I tell them. Many of them stutter out an, "Oh." Others look away. And still others tell me they gave up on religion years ago as if that cleared their bodies of inherited trauma.

Why is questioning God and Jesus a radical act? Why is reimagining the stories of Mary, Mary Magdalene, and Eve heretical? Why does it feel dangerous to believe in the "radical" Gospels that did not make it into the Bible? Why is it wrong to want my female body and blood to feel blessed and respected?

I imagine the Gnostic texts hidden in jars, buried in caves, simmering for centuries in darkness before reemerging into the light. My heart swells with profound gratitude for the errant monks who were, I am sure, told to destroy what had been oral and then written narratives of a Christ who knew divinity was in every human and loved paupers, lepers, and lords equally. The monks were true rogues. They said no. A Holy No can be just as powerful as the Holy Yes. Under the dark cover of night, they hid sacred words deep in the belly of Mother Earth.

Amen to all rogues who believe in the potential goodness of human beings, male and female. There are too many egos in the world, and throughout history, thirsting for power and hell-bent on conquer. For whom power is aphrodisiac and murder is a right. I can only get to Yes if I first utter, from the depths of my belly, a mighty *No*. I will not stop searching for truth, the whole story that confirms my place in the natural world. I will not accept the many lies I was taught in Sunday School and church. A gut-deep *No* is the only path to *Yes*.

◉

Slut. Feel your tongue against your hard palate when you say the word. Slut. Hear the hiss of shame when the word comes out of another's mouth. Shrink away from the word and feel a thick wall build itself across your middle, severing all that is above from all that is below. Bisected. Bloodless. Passionless.

Now say out loud the word "sacred." Feel the soft curl of your tongue and feel the air flow all around, mouth open slightly, loose and free. Go back and forth saying both words. Slut, sacred, slut, sacred. Hard. Soft. Demeaning. Empowering.

Slut has been used for centuries to hammer shame into female bodies. Images of slattern women are easy to conjure, while images of sacred women are tougher to come outside of mothers and virgins. Cartoon depictions of female power enhanced by bracelets and skin-tight clothing? Abundant.

Where are the female images of sacred sexuality, passionate intensity? It is up to all of us, the huge collective of female imaginations, to dream our own.

A memory returns from 1996 when I attend a three-week memoir workshop at Ghost Ranch in Abiquiu, New Mexico, led by Natalie Goldberg. About sixty of us, mostly women, meet in groups large and small to write the stories of our lives amid the same red rocks and animal bones of New Mexico that inspired the artist Georgia O'Keefe.

By the third week, the small group of five to which I had been assigned is tight. A deep friendship blossoms (four of us still alive write together today), cemented by writing together several times a day. On one of the last days, we hike into the surrounding red rocks to write and soak in our final hours of this sacred land.

I find a small curve of red earth out of sight of the others. Instead of writing, I plant my open palms into the dark red earth and stare at the red powder on my hands. On impulse, I strip off my clothes, rub that red dirt all over my body, lie back on the ground, and stare up into the vast bright-blue New Mexico sky. Sexual desire throbs and my fingers find their way to my clitoris. My red-dirt orgasm vibrates my body, intense, one of my best ever. I relax onto the ground, my body and soul bathed in sacred.

ROGUE GALLERY

As there's a use in medicine for poisons, so the world
cannot move without rogues.

—Ralph Waldo Emerson

HISTORY WAS MY least favorite subject in high school. I can still hear the drone of my eleventh-grade history teacher, Mr. Kirk, asking us why we study history and the only response he deemed correct: "To learn from the mistakes of our past."

Mr. Kirk was wrong. We live in a world that is pulled inexorably back in time to a good-old-day that never existed. We rarely learn from the past but instead airbrush and deny our way forward where mistakes and miscalculations hold us hostage.

A Rogue Gallery of Defiant Females is what I need most to remind me of my own power, and to inspire my creation of healing dream imagery. A Rogue Gallery of females whose life stories inspire me to shake and shimmy back to life long-dormant DNA in my own body.

I hit paydirt.

A few of the names I discover who set my DNA to spinning: Enheduanna, Inanna, Thecla, the Mesopotamian moon God named Sin, Christiana Morgan, Mary Magdalene, Pippi Longstocking, and Barbie. Role models extraordinaire who open my eyes and ears to the myriad ways to live life in a female body.

I offer dollops of who they were and how they lived in hopes you dig deeper through texts ancient and modern. My Rogue Gallery includes a poet, a Goddess, a fearless follower of the Apostle Peter, a moon god, a visionary and soulmate of Jesus, a Boston Brahmin, and two fictive characters. Feel their power inside the body, let them dance and dream you. Do not just learn their names. Soak them in and live the truths they model. May they, as they did for me, race your heart, root your feet, electrify your nerve-endings, sate your hunger and thirst. Do as Olympia Dukakis taught me so many years ago: feel and move their wisdom. Don't analyze. Engage.

I am so hungry, I thought for too many years. *I am so thirsty,* I whispered into dark nights in our cultural desert bereft of images and stories of female strength and creativity. My hunger and thirst led me deep into our ancestral history where I struck gold. So please, *Take, Eat. Take, Drink.* Seek and ye shall find your own Rogue Gallery of inspiration and hope.

◉

"My beautiful face is dust."

Her words are thousands of years old. Her anguish palpable, her rage justified. She wrote these words when female divinity was first shoved aside and male divinity began its mighty ascension. Her name is Enheduanna. She wrote of her beautiful face turned to dust more than two thousand years before the New Testament was written. A Mesopotamian poet and writer born about 2300 BC, Enheduanna was high priestess to the Goddess Inanna, Queen of Heaven and Earth. The one I moved and breathed with Olympia Dukakis.

Enheduanna is the first writer in recorded history, *male or female,* whose named works have been translated and preserved. Her poetry sings the praises of Innana and the glory of the divine feminine.

Hers is a voice from the time when goddesses were worshiped in temples built in their name. Goddesses who daringly dug deep and lived large lives of passion, wisdom, fertility, and courage. Enheduanna is the voice of female divinity. Free and unfettered. Loud and lusty.

Enheduanna is the voice of females whose bodies are revered and held most holy.

Enheduanna is the voice that breaks me open today, encourages me to feel the full force of life in a female body, traces of which still exist in my DNA. Remember, her poems insist, the time before female divinity was systematically eradicated, banned, and burned:

Lady of all essences, full light . . . clothed in radiance whom heaven and earth love . . . Oh primary one . . . Your fire blows about and drops on our nation. Lady mounted on a beast. An [a skygod in Mesopotamia] *gives you qualities, holy commands, and you decide.*

You decide. You choose. You have power. You have agency.

Tell me, my mother said to me when she invited me to trust the truth of my dreams. *You decide.*

As a high priestess to Inanna, Enheduanna is forced to bear witness when holiness and respect are stripped from Inanna. Enheduanna is the daughter of the Akkadian King Sargon. Inanna is not banished forever but the act demonstrates that female goddesses are dispensable. Male gods endure while female divinity exists at the whim of male leaders.

Enheduanna's voice rises from the ancient bones of history at the beginning of the end of female holy. Her lament portends the ascendence of sin-chocked female bodies with neither legal nor divine authority: *Now I am banished with the leper. Shadows approach the daylight, covering the day with sandstorm. My soft mouth of honey is suddenly confused. My beautiful face is dust.*

More than her face is ground to dust. Female rights to own prop-erty, engage in civics, and control their own bodies are also, slowly but surely, vanished by laws and creed that still thrive in abortion laws today.

Enheduanna brings the goddess Inanna to life in her poetry. In my imagination and dreams, I see Inanna pleasuring herself beneath the huluppu tree. An old white boy walks up to her, points a crooked finger, and demands she stop her sinful behavior. He pulls a paper from his pocked and shoves it in Inanna's face. On the paper, it is writ that the government has the authority to assert, in all female lives, decisions of life, death, and pleasure.

"Stop your lascivious behavior immediately," he demands. "You are breaking laws."

Inanna glares up at him, her fingers damp and fragrant, her cli-toris on high alert. She leans her head against the tree, moves fingers back to clitoris, and scores a throbbing, defiant, orgasm.

◉

What's the sin in this? The question haunts me for years and compels my search for the origin story of sin. Whose big idea was *sin* in the first place? Who fashioned sin like a poison arrow that pierces skin and wreaks havoc deep inside? And why did female bodies, more than male bodies, become the primary vessels of sin and shame?

Sin, of course, is a highly efficient weapon of mass control. Ladle it into human bodies, as they did thousands of years ago, and humans come crawling, begging and paying for forgiveness. The notion of sin was locked in concrete by the written word and has endured for centuries.

I imagine Roman and church leaders, the educated and literate, excited over the power of the written word. *With these words,* I imagine them chuckling, *I thee control*. *With these words*, they salivate, *I thee divide: literate from illiterate, ruler from slave, husband from wife*. *With these words*, they command, *I'm in charge and you shall obey*.

As I dig through sin's origins, I unearth an ancient moon god in Mesopotamia, way back in 3000–4000 BC, named Sin. One of a pantheon of gods revered by early humans whose origin stories, just like in the Bible, feature great floods, Gardens of Creation, and Inanna hanging on a meat hook for three days, instead of a cross, before resurrecting back to Earth.

Maybe Moses wrote Genesis, the first book of the Bible, in about 1400 BC, or maybe others wrote it somewhere between 400 and 500 BC. Whoever did write Genesis borrowed heavily from Mesopotamian lore. They keep the moon god Sin but strip him of moon face and craft him into a literary construct of major moral judgment. They decide Eve, who cycles each month with the moon, is the temptress and bearer of sin. *Let's blame it all on women*, I imagine Moses snickering as he blames Eve and seals sin inside female bodies where the two became one.

Sin the moon god is not simply drained of mystical radiance and phase-happy gravitational pull but is shaped into a deadly weapon for a single all-powerful male god in the sky. Here's what makes my heart happy: The soulful pull of the Moon on human bodies and imaginations endures. Sin, God of the Moon, refuses to be fully vanquished.

One must give credit for carving sin into such an enduring concept. Thousands of years later, we are still mired in sin. Humans spin through life on endless hamster wheels: sin, confess, repent, be blessed, pay up. Rinse and repeat. Some seek blessings through God and others through luxury goods and spa days. I can hear their justification: *I did bad and admitted it. Reward me*.

There is no such thing as sin, Jesus stated. Is there sinful behavior? Of course. Does sin wallpaper the innards of human bodies? Absolutely not. No sin. Nada. Zip. Let us claim divine authority in our hearts and allow sin, the nastiest three-letter word in human history, to morph back into the radiant beauty of the Moon. Radiance, not remorse, that soaks divinity into all.

◉

She refuses to marry, which is an illegal act in Iconium, Turkey, where she was born in 30 AD. She ignores pleas from her mother and fiancé to be a good girl. Behave. Follow the law. She sets out, instead, on a heroine's journey. Not at all like a hero's journey where slaying is essential. A heroine's journey requires full allegiance to inner knowing. Body-deep. Listening to and acting on inner authority—truth talk from the body.

Thecla, of a noble family, is inspired by the Apostle Paul who preaches of ascetism and sexual renunciation so that all passion is put in service to God. Thecla is a teenager when she hears Paul preach outside her open window. So mesmerized by his words of God, faith, charity, and prayer that she stays by her window, listening, not eating or drinking, for three days. She is engaged to be married to a prominent citizen. In those days, girls are owned by their fathers and then by their husbands, but Paul's words stir her rogue to life.

"No," she tells her mother, "I shall not marry."

"No," she tells her fiancé, "I shall not marry."

Paul is imprisoned for the words that Thecla takes to heart. Thecla bribes her way into the prison to sit all night near Paul and hear more. The next day, Paul is banished and Thecla is ordered to be burned at the stake, but God intervenes with rain that douses the flames.

Thecla baptizes herself in waters teeming with deadly sea-calves that are killed by lightning before they can eat her alive. She is spared death again when women of the community join forces to save her. Thecla is, for a third time, sentenced to death. This time she is to be ripped to death by wild lions and bulls. She is led naked into an arena, but all the women in town, who have come out to support Thecla, have drenched their bodies in rose, nard, and cardamom. The overpowering fragrance lulls the wild animals to sleep and, again, Thecla is spared.

Thecla's story echoes the myth of Inanna, which was written by Sumerians thousands of years before the story of Thecla. Both women willingly give up their jewels and external adornments. Both are stripped naked and forced to face deadly evils. Both return from their trials more courageous. Thecla lives to the age of ninety, preaching, praying, living in caves, sustained by her profound belief in God. Inanna returns to Earth as a revered goddess.

We all can die to old behaviors and reemerge into truer lives. Listen and learn.

◉

Christiana Morgan, a twenty-nine-year-old Boston Brahmin, writer, artist, and wife dreams and draws an archetypal female heroine's journey when she travels to Zurich for sessions with Swiss Analyst Carl Jung in 1926. Jung uses the therapeutic practice of active imagination where the analysand goes into a trance-like, active-dream state where images flow. Morgan's flow is formidable, and Jung is deeply affected by her imagination and intellect. So much so that he dubs her his muse and interprets and teaches Morgan's visions in a series of vision seminars he offered from 1930–1934.

One problem: Morgan neither agrees with nor grants Jung permission to use her active imaginations to teach others. She disagrees with Jung's notion of her as muse or dark feminine force.

To his credit, Jung brilliantly conceives the concept of the collective unconscious, the vast archetypal experiences of humans throughout time including love, hate, marriage, murder, and sin. However, his notions of collective female behaviors are severely narrowed by the era in which he lives and by his own life choices. A contemporary of Sigmund Freud, both men view females primarily as wives or lovers and treat female passions as more a mental disturbance than life force. To wit, Jung lives with his wife, Emma, and their five children in one house, and out back, in a separate structure, lives his collaborator and lover, Toni Wolff, a brilliant and intuitive visionary just like Morgan.

Google Morgan's images. Drink them in. Each one shows female power far more expansive than Jung's narrow notions of girls and women. Morgan draws images of females morphing easily between young and old, maiden and crone. She aligns female power with sacred snakes and alchemical fire, and she knows the female journey requires facing fear and venturing deep into places men are too terrified to enter.

Morgan's images depict a heroine's journey. She travels beyond the realm of Jung's narrowly conceived notions of females as muse, wife, lover, maiden, and crone. Morgan's images show a woman facing crones and hags, moaning and bereft. A female journey demands we not rely solely on brains or being so damned smart. A female journey requires us to do what terrifies men: claim and trust our instinct and intuition that is fertilized by our passion.

We must grieve, Morgan describes, from the depths of our being centuries of female containment. Our grief expressions are not quiet or polite but loud-mouthed and full-bodied moans over all that history has taken from us. She draws images of hundreds of female ghosts who have been raped and burned and tortured. *Face your terror,* Morgan's images demand. Howl and sweat our bodies into freedom.

Morgan conjures a blue-robed woman who demands she not speak. No words, just as Olympia instructed me. "I will show you," the woman says and walks into the center of a circle of female phantoms who clutch and tear at her skin, not unlike Thecla walking naked into an arena of wild beasts.

How did Morgan's rogue-journey turn out for her? She would serve as a lay analyst at Harvard's Psychological Clinic and coauthor, with Harvard's Henry A. Murray, of the *Thematic Apperception Text,* a widely used tool in clinical psychology. Murray, also married, became Morgan's lover. She was booted from Harvard in the 1960s because she had no credentials. Alcoholism and her troubled relationship with Murray did her in. She committed suicide at sixty-nine, but her images and words live on to inspire our own courageous transformation.

Morgan's biographer, the Jungian Analyst Claire Douglas, author of *Translate This Darkness: The Life of Christiana Morgan, the Veiled Woman in Jung's Circle,* writes that Christiana was "a powerful woman who never felt at ease with her strength." Her words and images, however, invite all girls and women today to feel at ease with their strength.

⊙

Pippi Longstocking leads the charge in the Rogue Gallery of my childhood. I adore her red braids jutting out from each side of her head, the cookie dough she spreads all over her kitchen, and her wide-roaming imagination. Pippi arrives in my life before I get my first Barbie doll. She sparks my imagination and leads me to range freely through the back alley exploring, building forts, digging in dirt, transforming a piece of plywood into a pirate ship, skinning my knees and getting dirty.

Barbie arrives when I am eleven, and I shove Pippi aside. My own Barbie is not an authentic Mattel product but is a cheaper knockoff that I love just the same. I still have her stored in her turquoise-blue "real" Barbie case with very few of the store-bought outfits, which were out of my parents' price range. But I have evening dresses, shorts, blouses, and a silky white robe sewn for Barbie by my grandmother.

As a teen, I packed Barbie in the back of my closet but keep alive my quest for the perfect outfit. Greta Gerwig's *Barbie,* which I have watched four times, convinces me of Barbie's strength. She is far more than her outfits. In fact, Gerwig's Barbie is a first-class rogue. Tearful emotions and existential angst fuel her longing to live a more dimensional life. Gloria, played by America Ferrera in the movie, is another rogue extraordinaire. She takes on her soulless, clueless corporate bosses and gives voice to the exhaustion of walking the Earth in female form.

Gloria's monologue captures the deadening dichotomies of female lives. Be beautiful-smart but never feel good enough. Aim for healthy not thin but always be thin. Lead but don't squash. Claim a career but always care more for others. Be an adoring mother but don't always talk about your kids. Be pretty but never a temptress of men nor threatening to other women. Stand out but always be grateful. And then there is the long list one must never do: get old, be rude, show off, be selfish, fall down, fail, show fear, get out of line.

Margot Robbie plays Barbie as a flesh-and-blood woman who gains what she wants most: a vagina, which can, of course, include a clitoris. The movie ends not with lovers embracing but with a woman proudly claiming her vagina and clitoris.

Barbie and Pippi complete my Rogue Gallery. Each one holds their own with Thecla, Mary Magdalene, Inanna, and all the others through time. Rogue Galleries know no limits: red braids, black-striped swimsuits, and all things pink complement long white robes and artist aprons. All are external trappings to the female hearts they cover. Female hearts with enormous strength stretch, reach, embrace, shatter, and open again. Our hearts know the language of rogue.

◉

Ocean breezes stir the heavy black fabric of the nuns' habits while their bare feet, sprung to life like freed animals, stride across the wet sand at the ocean's edge. I sit on the oceanfront balcony of our Airbnb startled by the sight of five nuns, four in full habit and one novitiate, walking with bold strides and big smiles near the water's edge on the beach in Carpinteria, CA.

Peter and I book seven nights at the Airbnb, a splurge after a year of pandemic prison, at an ocean-front condo on the top floor and at the far end of a three-story complex that sits smack on the Pacific Ocean. The ocean air, the sound of the surf when we sleep, and hours of beach walking, had, three days in, eased the pandemic-anxiety rooted in our bodies.

"Nuns on the beach," I whisper to Peter, beckoning him out to take a look. He was raised Catholic in the 1950s and attended all Catholic schools. The sight of nuns can still make the hair on his neck prickle with anxiety.

"They're barefoot," he notices immediately. "I've never seen a barefoot nun."

I snap a quick picture with my cell phone of the five barefoot nuns walking the beach on a Wednesday morning. When I look at the picture, I notice five seagulls clustered on the wet sand at the nuns' feet in the identical configuration as the nuns, two in front and three behind. The quick-snap picture is surprisingly well-composed: a broad stripe of deep blue ocean frames the top of the picture, two bold stripes of bright white wave-foam cut through the center just above the heads of five nuns and five seagulls all bordered across the bottom by a swath of sand.

When I share the picture with several friends, one of them notes that the picture looks like an ad for a new cocktail called Nuns on the Beach, a virgin version of the alcoholic drink Sex on the Beach.

The tableau of barefoot nuns and seagulls fills me with grace: divine female imagery drawn by sandy footprints. I imagine the nuns' bare toes, freed of the confines of sensible shoes and heavy habits, full-fleshed, wriggling in the ocean-wet, rooted in Mother Earth. Five smiling barefoot nuns, their toes in sensuous communion with wet sand offer a sweet dollop of all things female-divine.

Why, I wonder as I watch, *is female divinity buried beneath yards of dark fabric, looped round by beads and crosses, topped by wimpled faces?* I know nun garb has lightened up over the years, but the archetypal image of shrouded females remains vivid in our imaginations and legally enforced in other countries. Cloak it, shroud it, layer those bodies in fabric, hide the flesh.

The five nuns stir my imagination. Women who give over their lives to faith and service not unlike Thecla did with Paul. Their barefoot footprints leave their imprint on the sand and on my heart.

◉

Among my best talents, for which I will never win an Academy Award, is the beauty and brilliance of my dreams. A showcase of wisdom and creativity that unreel every night with technicolor brilliance. I have no idea why every human does not awaken each morning, bound out to get that bowl of Cheerios, and brag to their family: *You won't believe what I produced last night. Listen to this!*

My dreams overflow with roguish confidence and courageous acts. Moving pictures that convince me I am a shape-shifter and time-traveler unbound by space and time.

Listen to this! In my thirties, I produced a dream of a young mother. The action begins with me walking along the shoreline where a group of men busy themselves building something important at the edge of the water. I have no interest in what they are doing and walk inland. I come upon a woman who appears to be the leader of an ancient tribe of women whose numbers are dwindling with time.

It's midmorning, a clear blue sky with the bite of salt-air floating in a light breeze. A smattering of ancient tribe members relax in the shade of an ancient oak tree. A single picnic table, weathered with long planks for sitting on each side, sits in the center of the scene.

The leader walks over to greet me the moment she sees me and extends her child toward me so I can hold the baby girl. I am deeply moved that she trusts me with her child. I cuddle the baby and we sit together, side-by-side, at the table. Another woman brings a plate of pink and moss-green pasta beautifully arranged on a white serving platter.

We eat in comfortable silence. The baby on my right knee, the leader to my left. She wears a long white robe, belted by a rope. The wind blows her robe open below her waist, and I see her vagina.

Our vaginas look alike, I think to myself and glow with profound connection and gratefulness as the camera fades to black.

Another film spun from my dreams takes place on a late-summer night in Washington, DC, our bedroom windows open to cricket song, heavy humidity, and lush green fragrance. I am somewhere between dream and sleep when I get out of bed, stick my head out our window, and breathe deeply.

I am the summer night, my body tells me. I feel myself blend as one with crickets and lush green, a sensation that is both vivid and overpowering. With special three-dimensional effects, my skin tingles and heart beats hard as my porous body blends with the night. The voice-over proclaims: *She knows herself as part of the divine continuum, dark hush, lush green, her heart sung by crickets. One with all.*

My belief in dreams traveled directly from my mother's DNA to mine. Anne, my Jungian analyst, guides me back to that DNA, urging me to pay attention and believe. My own creative cells assure me I am writer, director, actor, and producer. My art, my vision is not smeared on canvas and hung for all to see in museums like the Uffizi. But it is art. Plain and simple. Every night I am gifted a blank canvas where I can love, laugh, dance, murder, howl, make passionate love, and blend with nature's powers.

I think I will buy myself a beret, wear paint-speckled pajamas to bed, and wait breathlessly as I fall asleep each night. What masterpiece shall I produce tonight? I have no idea where my dreams will take me, but I relish the roller-coaster ride. And, thanks to Anne and my mom, I gladly confer my own Academy Award for the moving images my rogue produces. Every morning over my bowl of Cheerios, I accept the award with a humble *thank you, thank you.* Savoring my unique eye, wisdom, and creativity, proclaiming myself a dreammaker of extraordinary talent. So are you.

LIVING ROGUE

Mystery is endangered but it need not be extinct.
—Mary-Louise Parker, *Dear Mr. You*

MARY MAGDALENE is the vision chick. The girlfriend you call with a big dream you need to share. She never laughs nor pooh-poohs. She simply, like my mom did for me so many moons ago, says, *Tell me.* She listens intensely and intently. She is the personification of eyes that see and ears that hear.

"How does vision work?" Mary in her Gospel asks Jesus. "The Savior answered and said, 'One does not see with the soul or with the spirit, but the *nous,* which is between the two, sees the vision."

Nous, from the Greek not French, has been translated in the Bible as "mind," which lands us in the bog of mind-body dualism. The radical tribes of long ago had no concept of a fault line drawn through the body: brain on one side and body on the other.

Meggan Watterson explains that in the early centuries, after Jesus was born but before the Bible was codified, *nous* translated as the "spiritual eye of the heart," the primary receptor in the body of direct knowledge and divine wisdom. *Nous* is among the best examples of the grist, guts, and glory that is wrung from human experience when narrowed by words that are then translated from one language to another. Once *nous* locked in as "mind," the poetic beauty and profound truth of all of us having a spiritual eye of the heart that linked body and soul vanished into the shadows of history and time.

Roman emperors were not invested in humans believing in their own felt-sense of divine authority. They were thrilled to translate all that Greek out of hearts. They knew how to control brains, enslave bodies. Working with church leaders, they blinded the nous, declaring that grace could only be conferred at the whimsy of robed men in dark confessional booths. I am certain the price of forgiveness rose steeply when massive gold-gilded cathedrals needed to be built.

Mary Magdalene's legacy is in explaining how to, in daily lives, reinstate the nous to its early glory. In fact, Mary Magdalene was also the how-to chick. I don't want to overstate her relevance to all females today, but take a read of her Gospel (it is short) and realize it is a how-to guide to live one's rogue: Trust your heart and belly. Blossom your soul, believe your visions. Know and trust yourself. Climb out of boxes of containment.

The male apostles were big on mansplaining Jesus's teachings while Mary's Gospel offers specifics on *how* to live one's life fully human and fully divine. *We can't just tell them they are human and divine,* I imagine her thinking. *We must explain how to pull it off.* Or, in Mary's words: *I will teach you what's hidden in you.*

She explains how our shaky egos can keep us mired in pain but can also guide us to healthier lives when balanced with soul. Egos are the scaffolding constructed outside our bodies by parents, siblings, friends, schools, churches, and culture. *This is how we see you and what we expect of you,* we are told again and again, and our egos try with all their hearts to conform to what others want and expect.

Ego is neither all bad nor all good. It is the part of us that lets us succeed at the details of daily life: paying the rent on time, never running out of gas. Ego is also the devil on our shoulder who lures us, always, toward wanting more and feeling victimized, insecure, jealous, and clingy. We were plopped on this earth in human form with egos that are vulnerable and fallible. Our main job is to integrate our shaky selves, wise souls, and rogue spirits into a seamless whole. Fully human, fully divine.

How do we do that? Mary's Gospel offers a seven-point plan on how to be human and divine. Not unlike today's articles that lure us in with five steps to a better sex life or three steps to a firmer stomach, Mary outlines seven specific behaviors that must be faced head-on. Nasty behaviors that keep us stuck.

The Nasty Seven: darkness, clinging, ignorance, excess, body obsession, sloth, and righteous anger. All of which thrive in female bodies today. I offer the following examples from my life on how these seven challenges reared their heads, pitched me into darkness, and made me forget my own soul.

◉

Power Number One—Darkness: I did not get the job that would have made my life perfect. A capstone of my career. I practiced my interview skills, reached out to mentors, had impeccable recommendations. This one had to be mine.

I did not get it. In its stead, darkness gets me.

Wine is my first response to darkness that night. I pour a big one. Fattest damn wine glass I can find in the house. Peter knows to stay upstairs, watch television, steer clear of the voracious darkness into which I dive head-first.

On the front couch, I gulp my wine, call a girlfriend who knows how much I wanted the job, and moan like Ereshkigal over the death of her husband:

Oh my insides, Oh my outsides, I wail. *I know, I know,* my friend reflects, *They chose the wrong person, they did.* I moan again, *I deserved that job.*

That night, Peter orders pizza, which I don't often eat, but that night, that night, I pick the largest piece of the pie, no plate, no fork, no salad with dressing on the side, open my mouth into the widest maw I can manage, and chomp off nearly half a slice. Tomato sauce dribbles down my chin but I don't care. Another two bites and all that is left is the crust which I finish off with glee. Pizza greases my fingers and cheeks and splatters on the couch. I grab another piece and suck it down.

Mary Magdalene names darkness as a major tool used by the ego to drag us down, shut out the light. Darkness, Meggan explains, is when we feel "separated, trapped, constricted, isolated, and alone. We have lost track of our deepest soulful love and connection with spirit and earth."

My soul hides upstairs with Peter that night. As far from me as she can get. Pizza and wine bloat my belly, reinforce my standard darkness mantra: I am fat and ugly, the mantra that darkness shoves my face into whenever it takes me down. In that place, my body fumes like Ereshkigal in the underworld, and I set the eyes of death on my very own body, murder it with pizza and wine. I fall asleep on the couch bathed in tomato sauce.

◉

Power Number Two—Clinging: I call her my inner Barbie. The part of me that springs into action the Easter Saturday I pedal my bicycle back and forth to Stimson's in search of red accessories for my black and white Easter outfit. I am twelve at the time and still play with my Barbie doll with her case of dresses, blouses, slacks, accessories, and shoes, tiny plastic wedges that slip on to her tiny triangular feet that force her to walk the world on tiptoes, unrooted.

My cousin Lanelle and I spend hours concocting events for Barbie marked mostly by changing her outfits. Barbie knows fashion. The spirit and ethos of Barbie remains with me during my corporate years and drives me to spend thousands of dollars on clothes and accessories: business pantsuits, casual attire, blouses, swimsuits, tennis outfits, and, of course, an array of long gowns for formal affairs. Each outfit requires accessories, the perfect shoes, purse, and matching shade of DKNY pantyhose.

My inner Barbie retires the weekend of the 109th Gridiron Club Dinner on March 21, 1994. As a corporate lobbyist, I attend a number of black-tie events, but the Gridiron is top of the food chain. A white-tie event, far superior to black-tie, attended by Washington's media and political elite with, most years, an appearance by the President of the United States who uses humor and satire to poke fun at himself and the media giants who cover him.

The Gridiron is much more than a single Saturday night dinner. The festivities begin on Friday evening at a dinner at the Bombay Club for all of the Times Mirror publishers and corporate executives who flew in to Washington to attend the dinner. The restaurant is a few blocks from the White House and an easy walk from my office at 18th and K. I buy for that night a silk jade-colored, shoulder-padded jacket that I pair with a white silk camisole, black crepe slacks, and black leather sling-back heels.

The next day is a luncheon at the *USA Today* building in Rosslyn for which I choose an off-white crepe skirt that hits just above my knee with a matching off-white short, fitted jacket, and beige sling-back heels. I am seated at a table that day with the documentary film maker Ken Burns whose nine-part miniseries, *Baseball*, would air that September on PBS. A lot of baseball talk at the table but the highlight is being introduced to the guest speaker, Hillary Clinton. She does not comment on my outfit, but I am starry-eyed to meet her.

The dinner Saturday night is held at the Capital Hilton Hotel. My dress: long and black with sparkles woven through, form-fitting but not clingy, no cleavage, strappy heels, and a sparkly clutch purse. Vice President Al Gore is the hit of the night when he is wheeled on stage during the comic bits on a handcart pushed by two workmen who prop him up next to the lectern like a wax museum dummy.

What I remember best is late Saturday night when I arrive home, peel off my pantyhose, hang the long sparkly dress in my closet, and wash my face. *I can't do this anymore,* I say to my reflection in the bathroom mirror. Three costume changes, all those accessories, different shoes for each outfit. Inner Barbie is exhausted; she wants out.

My body heaves a sigh of relief when I free it of waistbands, push-up bras, soul-sucking pantyhose, and pointy triangular shoes. The voice that says "enough" that night does not boom from inside of me like the one I hear years later at the shooting. This voice comes from my heels that are deliriously happy to be set free from a weekend of tiptoeing four inches off the ground. And from my toes, worn out after being wedged into triangular cages and forced to carry the brunt of my weight in shoes that elevate my heels to a worthless height. My breasts, underwired and molded into perky perfection, let out a hefty sigh when I set them free. My belly, flattened and contained since Friday in pantyhose prison, exhales a deep sigh of relief. I swear I hear my boobs and belly hollering, *I'm free! I can breathe!*

Enough, my body insists. Enough of being strapped, trussed, and squished. Enough clinging to acquisitions that might make me perfect. My soul, in full agreement with my body, bids my inner Barbie adieu. My days of perfection, expressed with sartorial precision, are nearly over.

◉

Power Number Three—Ignorance: "Don't you dare judge my marriage," my close friend shouts at me, fixing on me the eyes of death. She sits at a table on the side deck with the bay in full view across the street, the sun setting on what had been a nice day. She had been complaining about her husband, and I had heard enough.

I get up, move to the front deck, and sip a vodka tonic as the sun sinks below the water's edge. I can still hear her talking and, in one of my dumbest actions ever, I go back in. A grave mistake. This time I stand rather than sit, which fuels her perception, I know now, that I think I am better, standing as I am above her, looking down. A stance I took only because I didn't plan to stay long.

"We have been married a long time to these really good guys," I plead. "Maybe cut them some slack?"

The heat and humidity and the lingering effects of the pandemic are not helping on this trip. Indoor or outdoor restaurants? Stay indoors or go see things? I struggle with heat and she embraces it. Pandemic logistics and brutal humidity have frayed all our nerves.

"Don't you dare judge my marriage," she rages at me.

"I am not judging. It's just hard to hear how bad they are. I'm not attacking you," I say, defending myself, "I am defending them."

She is furious. I am stunned more than angry. I go inside. That evening, the silence is thicker than the humidity. I later apologize and tell her I did not mean my words as judgment. She says ok but does not apologize. We suffer through one more full day together before we fly home.

In my head, again and again, I explain, replay the conversation, try to reason and feel my own indignance at her anger. *Maybe I was judging*, I think to myself, but I wasn't. *I was defending*, I tell myself again and again. I am hooked. And stay hooked for months. We do not talk on the phone. No more Zoom calls for both of us and our husbands. She feels judged. I feel judged.

Both of us are in sore need of self-emptying love. I send an email on New Year's Day. *I miss you*, I tell her. She does not reply. I send a text in August, *Let's move on*. No reply. And then she reaches out in September. *Let's forgive and forget.*

The truth is she judged her husband for which I judged her, and she judged me for judging her for which I judged her again. A vicious circle of ignorant judging that strains our friendship even as we pledge to forgive and forget.

The power of ignorance is all about judging. Being judged, judging others. Ignorant behavior saps energy and mires me in the miserable land of blame.

"The soul does not judge," Meggan instructs. "Kenosis is a profound spiritual practice of self-emptying love so we do not judge ourselves nor do we judge others nor do we allow others' judgments of us to trigger or trap us." I sorely failed on that front.

◉

Power Number Four—Excess: In my twenties, I numb myself with sex. In my thirties and forties, I numb myself with work. In my fifties, I numb myself with finding and losing jobs. In my sixties, bullets and brain cancer numb me. Today, my numbing days are numbered. Excess is what culture wants from us every day—eat more, buy more, do more, be more. My zeal for excess has been softened because, hey, I am much closer to the end of my life than the beginning. My rogue advises every day: *Stop. Quiet. Listen.* Frenzy for more leaks out of my cells and leaves me in peace.

◉

Power Number Five—Forgetting: In ancient times, people wear long flowing robes that look pretty much the same for men and women. Prostitution is alive and well and women have few rights. Cleavage has not been invented. People are not saturated with advertisements featuring women's bodies to sell cars, beer, and guns. There is no pornography or online body-shaming. Webs back then are spun by spiders not technology. And yet, the realm of the flesh, where bodies take center stage and souls are banished to dusty corners, pops up at number five on the list of powers.

Body is everything in today's culture. All body, all the time. Weight, wrinkles, sags, bright white teeth, perfect hair, smooth elbows, painted toes, no-puff eyes, the perfect shade of lipstick, the thickest-longest lashes, the tightest abs, biggest muscles, bad breath, bunions. One's day is easily consumed by all things body, while soul is forced to bide its time in the corner to which it has been shoved. The United States has the largest advertising market in the world, cha-chinging in at nearly $240 billion. How many ads, on average, are we subjected to each day? Thousands and rising with all the pop-up computer ads, according to advertising experts.

Graven images abound.

Their aim: convince us to spend money on putting food into, taking pounds off of, clothing, clipping, polishing, legally drugging, and keeping in top shape these bodies of ours. Our economy and culture link inextricably into an unholy, financially ruled alliance that reveres body obsessions as all holy.

Soul? Did someone say soul? Just a moment, I'll get out of my expensive car, smooth my designer clothes, take a swig of my bottled water, which, by the way, is infused with antioxidants, and go meditate. I'm up to five minutes now!

◉

Power Number Six—Sloth: Here's to my inner sloth. The counterpoint to my addiction to perfection. The one I turn to when I wear out from all the striving and perfecting: computer solitaire, reruns of *Friends, Frasier,* or *West Wing.* My sloth thrives on solitary card games and an endless loop of reruns.

I do want to change, I tell myself. Maybe someday I'll be perfect. Pure of thought and deed, sleek and strong of body. Never sloth-like. Look at me, please look at me. But my sloth rears its head at least a few times a month. *Ah, come on,* she lures: *You've earned it, tune in, turn off the world, it's a jungle out there and aren't you tired of thinking, worrying? Take a load off. Come ride the sloth-mobile. Now isn't that nice?*

◉

Power Number Seven—Rage: Wrathful anger is righteous anger, and righteousness has landed our world into a whole heap of death and pain. Righteousness: the quality of feeling morally, justifiably, absolutely correct. So many have been slaughtered with righteous abandon. If I am morally right and you disagree with me, then you can only be morally wrong, which grants me the moral right to hate, wound, or murder you.

I know righteous anger, and my favorite place to let it rip has been Las Cruces, New Mexico, known as The City of the Crosses, forty-six miles northwest of El Paso, bordered by the Organ and Doña Ana Mountains. The Rio Grande runs through the valley, gracing it with wide swaths of bright-green respite from the surrounding Chihuahua Desert.

Peter and I reach Las Cruces, our third stop there in as many years, at about four in the afternoon after a nine-plus hour drive from Austin where we had gone to see Amanda, my brother Don's oldest daughter, graduate from the University of Texas. Our visit with Amanda, Emily, and Hunter, Don's three grown children, was beautiful, painful, and poignant, fraught with emotion. Don died before he could see his oldest daughter graduate from college while his only grandchild, Cember, Amanda's daughter, holds her right hand high in the Texas Longhorn salute as she watches her mom accept her diploma.

We are hot and tired from the long drive and exit I-10 at the first blue sign listing nearby hotels. We settle for a Hilton and lug our things from car to room, crank up the air, and sit quietly, waiting for the highway buzz in our bodies to quiet.

"Do you still want to go find something to eat?" Peter asks me.

"We could order pizza if you're too tired to get back in the car," I say.

"I thought you wanted to go out," he counters.

We are off. A stupid conversation between two hungry people enflamed by fatigue. We know the fight well from our years of marriage . . . Say what you want; I did, you don't listen. I listen fine, why can't you choose an option and stick with it? We know our lines by heart. It is also a fight we tamp down, reach a temporary peace, share a nice meal and then, boom, here it comes again when we are back in the room.

I feel righteous anger that night. I know I am right and he is wrong. About what, I am not certain, but I know I am on the side of the angels. My poor-me victim rears her head. Neither of us sleep well but we manage to talk our way to peace the next morning before getting back into the car. We are mostly silent as Peter drives, and I scroll mindlessly through Facebook. A random Eckhart Tolle quote a friend posted on Facebook page punches me in the stomach: *When you complain, you make yourself the victim. Leave the situation, change the situation, or accept it. All else is madness.*

I read the quote as I stare out the window at the dry, unchanging landscape. I have been half sulking as I scroll Facebook, feeling sorry for myself that Peter is so mean, knowing the fight is all his fault. Tolle's message gives my self-pity a swift kick: *Get over it. Grow up.* I have never thought of myself as a victim but have been quick over the years to accuse Peter of acting like a victim. Tolle's words shine their light directly on me.

Oh, my god, I know this is my fault. Poor little me. I need to fess up to my own self-righteous victim if I ever hope to let her go. In the middle of the Chihuahuan desert, on a dusty April morning, I stare down my inner victim and release her into the desert heat.

I gotta tell Peter, I think to myself. *This whole mess is on me.*

I look over at Peter, who stares straight ahead down the long white line of I-10. I have always loved the slope of his nose, the crisp blue of his eyes, the soft indent between his shoulders where I love to lay my head, soaking in the cool flesh of him. My heart softens and anger dissipates.

"I need to tell you something."

"What?" he asks, his voice gruff.

"I am sorry. I am really sorry. I have called you out on your victim behavior so many times, and never admit or realize how much my victim gets in our way."

"What are you talking about?" he asks.

I explain the Tolle quote, the sense of release in my body when I acknowledge my role in our fights, and release my self-righteousness.

"Have you ever wondered why we always fight in Las Cruces?" I ask.

"Not really."

"Las Cruces is the cross," I say. "I keep climbing up on the cross, feeling sorry for myself, feeling like a poor victim. It's my fault. My 'poor me' picks the fights. I see it; I get it. I am ready to never climb up on this bloody cross again!"

Peter's eyes soften. He reaches for my hand. "Tell me more."

I have spent thousands of dollars on therapy since Mom died in 1978, and not one therapist has called out my poor-me victim. It is a relief to face this toxic part of me, and when I do, the heaviness in my body lifts and my tears dry up. When I am trapped in notions of victimization, my rogue energy is stifled. I am mired in the present—a puppet being danced by strings from the past. On this trip, I finally acknowledge my victim and release self-righteousness into desert sun and dirt. My rogue applauds loudly from a place deep inside my heart.

◉

On a recent April night, the Full Pink Moon crowns above the Santa Catalina Mountains as a slim silver line that expands moments later into a bright orb in the night sky. A supermoon, the experts say, and I spread a beach towel on our flagstone patio to moon-bathe naked in the rose-hued light.

The day's heat huddles in the flagstone beneath my back while radiant moonlight tingles my skin. I open my mouth wide for a moment and stick out my tongue to catch more silvery rays. I am Wonder Woman at my recharge station.

Moonlight is not the only thing alive beneath the skin. I have learned that moonlight beams my rogue to life. *Feeling insecure?*

Darkness got you depressed, hopeless? Take your body outside on a moonlit night. Soak moon rays body-deep and feel the radiance clear you out.

As I lay in the April moonlight, joy bubbles through me. The many dragons I have befriended along the way have transformed who I am in the world. Their befriended bodies have fertilized me into a truer version of myself. Moonlight, in fact, is the best fertilizer there is to grow darkness into light and trauma into courage by erasing imaginary lines between body, brain, and soul.

"Bring love to our brokenness," Meggan Watterson tells us is a main message of Mary's Gospel. Moonlight heals my own brokenness. A beacon of love that radiates through every human being, no matter their station in life. Free and there for the absorbing.

ELEMENTAL

The most beautiful and most profound experience is the sensation of the mystical. It is the power of all true science. He to whom this emotion is a stranger, who can no longer wonder and stand rapt in awe, is as good as dead. To know that what is impenetrable to us really exists.

—Albert Einstein

WHY DO I FEEL unworthy to claim divine connection I know and feel in my body? Why do I hesitate to claim divinity in female faces? Why do I override the eye of my heart?

One easy answer: Fire.

I can sit mesmerized staring at burning logs for hours. I love the smell, crackle, and transformative power of fire. But fire also scares divinity out of me. Hundreds of thousands throughout history have been burned at the stake for witchcraft and heresy. Hundreds of thousands. Throughout history. I would be a fool not to harbor fears of fire as punishment for roguish behavior.

I see her led through the streets, hands bound, long dress dragging through the dirt. Her tangled hair hasn't been brushed for days, weeks, no baths in the dungeons where she has been chained.

This could be you, the authorities warn as they parade her before the townspeople. A lesson here. *Be afraid, be very afraid. We have power over your body, your life. We shall tell you what is right and what is wrong to believe and feel. We know best, you know nothing whatsoever worth knowing. We value obedience over imagination. We will tell you how to live your life. Our authority overrides the knowledge you glean from your direct experience of life. Wipe that direct knowing from your stupid senses. We are the law.*

She is marched to the town center, toward a stake planted in the middle of logs and twigs. See her tied there. Watch him strike the match, light his long torch, saturated in all things flammable. See flames spark in the logs and twigs beneath her feet. See the flames lick and singe the lower hem of her dress.

See the smoke start to rise. Pray, deep and hard, she passes out. Fast and quick. Let the heat and lack of oxygen suffocate her. Let the poisons in the smoke choke her to death. Let the loss of all the liquid wet of her wipe away her consciousness.

What we cannot see is fire devouring her from the inside out, contracting her soft tissue, sizzling and shrinking her fat and muscle. What we can see is the fire sear her skin, the twitch of her joints flexing beneath the flame, contorting, away, away, trying desperately to find solace, salvation. Tight ropes prohibit her charred joints from contorting into prayer.

Hundreds of thousands, throughout history and even in our United States, dead by fires justified by heresy or witchcraft.

I am afraid. I am very afraid. The fires of history were lit to keep me obedient, to burn out of me divine connection and love. My rogue reminds me that alchemical fires melt ancient chains. I can set myself free.

◉

Marilyn Moon is a dear high school friend whose parents foster children with severe disabilities. Many afternoons after school, Marilyn and I work with one of the young girls, Patty, who has cerebral palsy. Patty's arms, hands, legs, and feet curl inward toward her body. She cannot walk, sit, or feed herself. We place her on her back on a table with Marilyn on one side and me on the other. Each of us gently, carefully, move her arms and legs back and forth, one side then the other, replicating a crawling motion to repattern Patty's brain.

I am reminded of Patty in June of 2020 when I turn to swimming to survive the isolation of the pandemic and the fires that burn nearly one hundred and twenty thousand acres in the Catalina Mountains. Ignited by lightning strikes, the fires slash through the belly and over the tops of the Catalinas. Our backyard offers a front row seat to the flames as they eat their way across the drought-stricken mountain, boosted by hot winds and high temperatures.

I have always been a runner, hiker, solid-surface human born in the earth sign of Capricorn. The flames, heat, and pandemic confinement leave me parched, desperate for water, and I, a mediocre swimmer at best, take to the water immediately. Relief floods my body the minute I ease myself in and drop below the surface of the outdoor pool at our town's recreation center. No virus can reach me underwater; I am a slick-skinned guppy free of the bonds of earth.

I rent my own lap lane for fifty-five minutes and begin swimming most days. The rhythm lulls as I stroke right, left, right, left, back and forth, back and forth, again and again. Memories of Patty and Marilyn return, and I know I am repatterning my own brain, balancing the right and left lobes.

On my back, abs tightened so my butt lifts slightly in the water, the cloudless Tucson sky spreads above me. The blue water buoys me as the blue sky domes my watery world. On one morning, a sliver of the waning moon hangs directly overhead just as the sun ascends over the Catalina Mountains to the east. The moon and sun happily share the morning sky.

Wearing earplugs, swim goggles, and a tight royal blue swim cap, I submerge my head and tune into the sounds beneath the water. The stroke of my hands through the water, the paddle of my feet, and me, submerged and slithering. I chug and churn through the hollow echo of me in the womb-like confines of the pool.

Beneath the water, I imagine the watery world that pulled and folded me in my mother's womb, grew me from seed and egg to fetus to human. Liquid divinity. As I swim, swallows swoop overhead. My mother's favorite bird, the ones we drove to San Juan Capistrano every March to witness their return. Of course, there would be swallows. The blend of water, Mother, swallow, and womb stills my heart.

A favorite moment in the pool is when I flip to my back, stare up at the vast Tucson sky, and float. Savasana in the water—the yoga pose of complete relaxation—quiets my brain and invites my imagination to wander. If I flail, I sink. When I release, extend my arms and legs long in the water, and relax my shoulders neck and head as if the water were a pillow, I am held.

Water soothes my genes, reminds them of their womb-deep origins, and sings a song of strength and courage that shimmers through my every cell.

◉

Smoke shrouds the Catalina Mountains and holds us valley-dwellers in a chokehold. I sit inside our living room, doors closed, room fans whirling. As if the pandemic had not already sealed us away.

"Stir it up," I pray to the fans as I feel the breath in my body held hostage by a fire lit by lightning seven days earlier.

The flames of this fire are driven by high winds and temperatures, worsened by climate change, marauding through the canyons and ravines of the Catalinas with reckless abandon. North to south. East to west. Flitting with whimsy and caprice like the most beautiful woman at a ball flirting her way from one suitor to the next.

The news is also full of breath-related stories. Towns and cities banning chokeholds. Hospitals running short, yet again, of respirators. Breath demands our attention with its scarcity. If we want to breathe on this planet, we better wake up.

In the months after the shooting and my brother's death, I could not breathe except in shallow neck-up gulps. I felt too terrified to inhabit my body after witnessing so much death and destruction of too many bodies of people I loved.

"I can't breathe," George Floyd begged with his face in concrete and a knee on his neck. "I can't breathe," I sobbed to Amy as grief clogged my body. "I can't breathe," I cried to my husband as fire sucked oxygen out of our smoke-stoked valley.

We know breath best when it is denied us. The breath of too many of us over too many centuries has been forced from our bodies by a knee of someone who, allegedly, was there to protect us. Breath resurrected me from grief and pain. Breath roots me in the now. Breath is the life source of my internal organs. Deep inhales and deep exhales send messages of courage to my DNA. Shift and breathe. Breathe and shift.

◉

Mountain pose demands one stand still and quiet. Stand tall, feet parallel and rooted on all four sides—pinky toe, big toe, both sides of the heel. Soften knees, unclench glutes, shoulders up and back, open up your heart, chin tipped up so throat, third eye, and crown are open, receptive. Wiggle your fingers and feel the sensation. Root through your feet. Close your eyes, deepen your breath—inhale through the nose, side body to belly. Exhale just as deeply belly to nose. Be the mountain. Just now. Fully release into your body, your breath. Feel your mountain power. You in your body with your breath. Rooted strength. Feel the openness across your chest, roll your shoulders up and back, open your heart center. You are safe. Let your imagination and spirit soar. Hold there a minute, fat and sassy, fully present. Your body. Your breath. Rooted and alive.

⦿

Felidae. Bobcat. The resilient survivor of a family line where too many of your kin trundle toward extinction. You, ferocious feline, drop into our backyard for a Sunday morning visit.

You arrive over the top of a six-foot stucco wall and drop beneath the Silver Oak at the edge of our lagoon pool surrounded by rosemary, Sago palms, bougainvillea, Mexican Bird-of-Paradise and stately Queen Anne palms. An island of desert green lured out of the Sonoran earth by too much water.

I startle and stare, entranced by your gray-brown pelage. We eye each other long and close, and I let my fear suspend for just a moment. I imagine running my fingers through your spotted fur, breathing in the hot-toothed breath of you, feeling your fang and claw pierce my soft pink human skin. Kundalini, come to mama. You are one hot animal.

Fear wins out in the end. I leap up, spilling *New York Times* and Kenyan coffee to the ground as I race toward the safety of the kitchen door. You sit stone-still, unfazed by my human blithering, bored even, by who or what I might be. The acuity of your night-vision eyes reduces me to insignificance.

I know bobcats only from books I have read about wildlife in the

Sonoran Desert. You roam large and free through our arid land and just as easily inhabit the coniferous forests of the Pacific Northwest, the wetlands of Florida's everglades, and the cold northern forests of New England.

My brain had memorized facts and figures of you but this Sunday morning, my blood leaps at the flesh-and-blood you, stirring a part of my own DNA that must, somehow, through the intricate dance of evolution and alchemy, share a thread or two of the Felidae name.

From the kitchen window, I call to Peter to share in the wonder. We watch you leap, helicopter-like, straight up into the upper branches of the Silver Oak. You pause, stretch full on your haunches like pictures I have seen in the pages of *National Geographic*, lingering among the high limbs for a long moment or two, until you drop, just as suddenly, to the other side of the wall.

You vanish.

A feeling stirs deep inside of me, like a taste or smell I cannot name, but is there, lodged marrow-deep in my own blood and bone. A hint that I once lived as you still live, unbound by fence or leash, untethered by appointments and plans, marching to the rules of time led only by pangs of hunger and the need for sleep.

I open the back door, run to the fence, and stand on the bench so I can peer over the wall. Rogue in animal skin. I see no trace of you, just stretches of wild desert in the silence of a Sunday morning.

◉

The body never lies, but we neither listen to all it has to say nor trust what it tells us. Our bodies speak loudest about the food we shove down. In fact, appetite is the mother-tongue of the body. Listen, learn. No more counting, weighing, measuring every bite. No more comparing, loathing, or denying. Close your eyes, sink down into that beautiful body, and let it tell you what will best sate the instinctive brilliance of its appetites.

Among the most important messages my DNA needs to hear and respond to is that my appetite is my own. Mine. Not my mother's, not my cousins', not my girlfriends', or sister's. Mine. All mine.

Color, texture, fragrance, and taste: the gods and goddesses of our appetites. Take, eat; take, savor. You know the tastes your body prefers: Salty crunchy? Sweet and sour? Umami? I know what tasted best to me as a kid in my elm tree but all the counting of calories and carbs severed the connections between appetite, taste, and my brain. Our connections between instinct and bodily needs have been broken.

My stomach has always been my weakest internal organ. A hater of spicy food, cucumbers, and green peppers. *I would like that mild,* I always say in Thai, Indian, or Mexican restaurants. My appetite, however, has never felt to be my exclusive domain.

A memory: I eat lunch with my cousin Lanelle, whose mother, my Aunt Madge, is Mom's older sister and only sibling. My mom and Aunt Madge have a testy relationship, poisoned by jealousy and tainted by long-held competition. They had generously passed the shit that plagued their relationship along to me and my cousin Lanelle, who is six months younger than me. My mom was tall and thin and Aunt Madge short and rounder. Lanelle and I inherited the same body types as our mothers, which means the undigested-and-never-dealt-with-shit between my mom and aunt was bequeathed to Lanelle and me.

My mother once said she would not wear a beautiful white silk blouse to my aunt's house because it would make Aunt Madge feel bad. I was taught at a young age: Never do anything that might make another feel bad even if it makes you feel good. The feelings of others trumped my own needs and desires, always and forever.

We are about nine years old the day Lanelle and I are eating lunch together in the small breakfast nook at her house. I stare down at my creamed tuna on toast and feel too full to eat another bite. I look over at Lanelle, who is eagerly downing her lunch, and then back at my plate. I force myself to finish because I think that if I eat less than Lanelle, she will feel bad.

As an adult, I dream of Lanelle, hugely fat, unlike real life. She is seated on a throne and I am her loyal liege. "Feed me," she demands, her fat rippling over the edge of the seat and wedging its ways through the arms of the throne. "Feed me," she says again, and I run to grab a loaf of bread, thick with butter, that she gobbles down, streaks of yellow smearing her mouth and cheeks.

Another dream: A beautiful young woman is locked inside a cage so small she cannot stand up. She is on all fours, her long brown hair sweeping the floor. I stand outside the cage, tossing bits of food at her.

My shit.

And then, on a beautiful morning in October 2021, my sigmoid colon screams for attention. It's the lower third of my large intestine, connected to my rectum, the space for fecal matter to hang out until elimination. Stated more simply: the parking place for shit before I dump it back into the world.

My own shit turns streaming brown on a Friday morning. Knowing there is no way I can teach my yoga class, I madly text for a substitute while dashing back and forth to the bathroom. The diarrhea lasts three days and is accompanied by a burning sensation in the lower left side of my belly. At first, I do not connect the diarrhea with the burn and think I might have a hernia. My doctor orders a sonogram that shows nothing at all. My bowels calm and the burning subsides for a month before it all comes crashing back.

This time, I see the nurse practitioner I have seen for years who listens to my symptoms and immediately nails it as diverticulitis in my sigmoid colon.

"We'll get you on an antibiotic and the pain should clear up in a few days," she tells me. She also says I need, for at least a few weeks, to eat only white and bland: rice, oatmeal, broth, maybe a scrambled egg. I nod and fill the prescription and feel like I have landed in my dream of being kidnapped by that car full of men.

I have a long and torrid relationship with shit in my life. In my younger years, I hated and was embarrassed by the urgency and sounds of shit, the fart and stink of it. Constipation has long plagued me, and some part of me believed I would never be in a long-term relationship because I could not fart in front of someone else. Throughout the sleeping-around years of my twenties, no matter the hour, I roused myself from warm beds to go home after sex so I could fart and, of course, shit the next morning. I needed my bed, my bathroom. Elimination was a source of shame, an alien part of my body I denied and repressed. Inconsistent and at odds with beauty.

Fraught.

The morning after seeing my nurse practitioner, I eat a bowl of Thai jasmine rice, the antibiotics already easing the burning sensation. I am grateful for the diagnosis. Diverticulitis. I have a name and proof of my years of "tender tummy." *From now on*, I think to myself, *my stomach is mine*. I will never again look outside myself to decide what I will and won't eat. I can and will say, no thank you, I'm done, I can't eat sausage and hate spicy food. No thank you, I can't. I have a diagnosis. Forget nice, forget polite, I'm taking care of me first. My loyal-liege days are over. It turns out I did not have diverticulitis but that does not take away my awareness of my tummy as all mine, a recognition that lets me release old shit.

My Stomach, My Self.

I have a DVD of my brother Don, strumming his guitar and doing his best Mick Jagger imitation singing "Sweet Virginia" by the Rolling Stones. I find the DVD in my closet and watch Don mug for the camera, strum his guitar, and belt out the lyrics. I have watched the DVD many times over the years since Don's death but this time I listen more closely to the lyrics. My dear brother reinforces what I know I must do: wipe all my old shit clean away.

◉

We eat mystery every day. The mystery of seeds planted in brown earth that poke their small green heads above the surface of all that dirt. Add sunshine and water, no need to stir, and watch those heads grow sturdy and tall. See them beget vegetables and fruits and grains. Hallelujah. Food is our daily dose of mystery. How on Earth do those tiny seeds and seedlings root and grow and beget?

Too many girls and women, including me, carry stomach wounds. The Achilles heel of the female body. Our deepest soul-wound that plunges us into lethal relationships with the life-source of our human bodies. Food.

Here is my prayer: Every time a female stomach growls with hunger, the owner of that stomach might stop a moment, close her eyes, let mystery and wonder fill her body so that when she responds to that growl, she pays close attention to taste, texture, color, and smell. That's it. No diet book needed. Know your own hungers. Know you can satisfy them. Food speaks the mother-tongue of your body.

Who was the brilliant one who realized one of the best ways to go after females to dilute their power was to take aim at our appetites, our hungers? Someone recognized hunger could be transformed into the root of female vulnerability, self-hatred, and insecurity. Advertisers certainly picked up on this core tenant of our culture with thousands of images and messages to make females believe they do not know how to eat to suit their own needs. *Let's get them obsessing about their outsides until they lose sight of and connection to the power of their insides.*

Judging hands literally snake their way inside female bodies, with fables involving apples, demanding we question, suppress, and rewire our hungers so that we are afraid to admit hunger, stuff or starve, eat when we are tired, sleep when we are bored, screw when we are lonely.

Changing our relationship with food requires tough talk to our DNA and a commitment to reclaim the mother-tongue of our bellies. We must assert autonomy and mastery over our hungers with consciousness and persistence. No more measuring and weighing but dive, instead, into the joy of growing, eating, sharing, and loving food. Joy, joy, joy.

We can create a world all of us can stomach.

LOVING MY BROKEN

Character cannot be developed in ease and quiet. Only through experience of trial and suffering can the soul be strengthened, ambition inspired, and success achieved.

—Helen Keller, author, lecturer, and political activist

ROY ROGERS galloped his golden palomino Trigger out of our black and white television set and into my little-girl heart. Roy had high cheek bones and a smile just like my daddy. Each time Trigger reared on his hind legs, I imagined Roy swooping me up on Trigger's back and riding off into western adventures.

My equine love vanished in my teens when I was thrown from two different horses. Terror replaced awe for this brilliant animal at about the same time I shoved aside my innate instinct to focus on my outside appearance.

Horses have been around for fifty million years compared to humans' five to six million. They are prey not predators, which means they have successfully survived their way through giant sloths and dinosaurs. Do you know how much instinct it takes to evolve your existence through a host of massive predators? My answer is "yes," since rogue is all about evolving through a host of predators hell-bent on keeping females small and silent.

Horses have survived thanks to their heightened limbic system that radiates awareness of their environment from a half-mile radius. They can feel the vibration of the Earth through their hooves, which are connected to their heart by a main artery running down their front legs. Horses communicate and feel each other through space entirely through body language. For the record, brain researchers have found women tend to have more neural connections between the limbic system and the front part of the brain, which makes us better at managing emotional reactions. Females, most assuredly, have more horse-sense.

It had been more than thirty years since I had been face-to-face with a horse, and I liked it that way. Until I meet Bobbi, a horse whisperer at a ranch in Whitefish, Montana, where I was attending a writer's workshop led by the author Laura Munson. Bobbi was invited by Laura to speak with us about the power of equine therapy and offer sessions for anyone interested. No need to mount a horse, Bobbi promises, just hang out and soak in horse wisdom.

Tears sting my eyes as Bobbi describes the gentle wisdom of horses. "Horses see right through you," she explains. "They only do real."

I need this, I think to myself, raising my hand to volunteer while admitting to Bobbi and the other writers, "I am terrified of horses."

"That's good," she tells me. "You admit it. Too many people pretend they aren't afraid. Horses don't like fakes."

I am eager to release not only my horse fear but also the anxiety-residue in my body from the shooting. Eight years have passed since I watched my friends shot and killed but that is not enough time. Three months before meeting Bobbi, another gunman in an El Paso Walmart murdered innocent men, women, and children shopping on a Saturday morning. Another Saturday morning of shopping, about the same time as the Safeway shooting.

My PTSD flares.

Two weeks after the El Paso shooting, I stop by our neighborhood Target to buy a few items including a birthday card for a friend. I am fine as I approach the glass-doored entrance until a pregnant woman walks in front of me followed by a man with two small children. Images of the innocent families killed in El Paso flash through me. Maybe the name of the store—Target—adds to my fear. Don't know. I do know I spike, big time.

Come on, I tell myself. *This is Target, not Safeway or Walmart. Let it go.*

I take three deep breaths and make myself walk inside but immediately begin to scan. To the right a young man leans against a wall. Is he looking for victims? Is the bulge in his shirt pocket a gun? Does he look crazed?"

"Breathe," I tell myself. "Keep walking."

The aisles are stacked nearly to the ceiling with merchandise. Nowhere to hide. Nowhere. I did not realize how exposed a person is in a store. No crannies to crawl beneath, just walls of stuff piled from floor to ceiling, barriers that corral shoppers into easy target range.

Maybe I can hide in the middle of that rack of blouses, no, that wouldn't work, he would see me. How far to the bathroom? I can barricade myself in. No, that would be awful listening to others being killed. And he could shoot off the lock and then murder me huddled by a toilet. Do I want to die huddled by a toilet? The undeniable truth that I am prey overwhelms me.

In the greeting card section, I grab a birthday card and find a checkout line with only one woman who appears to be buying a single gift bag. *I've got this, I can do this.* The bag, it turns out, is not empty. She fishes out a plastic toy, cards, wrapping paper, a bar of candy. *Hurry up, I am losing it, please just hurry,* I want to scream but just stay silent, twitching.

"No bag, thanks," I say to the checker when it is finally my turn. I pay and bolt for the door. In my car, a scream explodes out of me, scratching my throat and vibrating my windpipes.

My trigger list includes the obvious: fireworks, loud claps of thunder, any sudden noise, and, of course, butterflies. Now I must add Saturday morning shopping and merchandise barricades in store aisles. My list is precious to me. I recite it often, like a rosary, hoping, if I repeat the list enough times, I might rub the beads of trauma down to nothing and be forever safe.

But horses? Not on the list. An hour before my equine appointment as we all eat lunch, my anxiety spikes. The Target experience is too recent and the anxiety it sparked now bleeds into my long-held fear of horses. Horses, bullets, murdered friends mingle into a toxic-terror mix that spikes me big time. No way am I strong enough to face my old fears of horses while still chock full of anxiety from my Saturday morning at Target. I rush out of the lunchroom in desperate need of fresh air.

One of my new friends from the workshop, an osteopathic doctor, follows me outside. She hugs me close as I sob, holds my hand, and walks me to her room.

"Sit," she tells me. I do what she says, as grateful as I was the morning at Safeway to do whatever anyone tells me. I sit, hang my head toward the ground. My tears ease and deep breaths calm my body.

"Can you feel your legs?" she asks as she presses her hands into my calves.

"Can you feel your feet? Do you feel the ground?" She presses my feet to the ground.

"Yes," I whisper, physically wresting my body back from trauma's invasive hands.

I know, firsthand, I am prey, and the terror of my vulnerability swallows me whole. I do not force myself to face the horses that day, but they work their magic on me from a distance. I do not repress or pretend away my anxiety. My sobs erase any pretense or persona. Trauma is my truth. I will never fully heal from the bullet-terror I witnessed, but the horses accept me as I am: broken, imperfect, but still alive.

◉

I blame this rant on the author John Updike. He wrote that "after a while you begin to long for the chirp and swing and civilizing animation of a female character." He was writing about a Booker Prize winner and zinged that in. Too many female characters over too many hundreds of years have been reduced to "chirp and swing," and thrust into "civilizing." Updike's word lands a punch. Enough. He pisses me off. So here's to you, Mr. Updike.

I am Jacquelyn Louise Jackson. Say my name. Use every syllable. It is not arrogance that leads me to claim the full Jacquelyn of my birth; it is not hubris that has me discard Jackie, the name of my east coast self, a roiling ball of passion and insecurity I strove mightily to tame and civilize. Jackie is the name that those who have known me the longest have the most trouble discarding. They come out with Jackie and, uh, I mean Jacquelyn, slow and awkward as if the extra syllable has lassoed their tongue.

Say my name. I reclaim my full name when we move to the Sonoran Desert. My rogue thrives as Jacquelyn and is muted by Jackie. My rogue demands I stand tall in my full name and takes great umbrage with "chirp" as a descriptor of female voice. Jacquelyn cannot be chirped, will not civilize, and does not walk this Earth to animate men. Jacquelyn thrives in the marrow of my being as color and light. Jacquelyn is the summer evening, star and thorn, a carnelian inquisitor eager to take back the world.

"Come outside," the sky demands as I sit on my couch staring at the *New York Times* crossword. I obey, drawn by a kaleidoscopic swirl of light and mountain. I stand in Mountain pose facing into the rising eastern Sun to soak in its dawning vibrance. In the chill morning air as I stand and stare, the light, uncontained, shifts, shimmies, morphs. The same energy I imagine inside my DNA. The dance of living spirit that invites me to spread my wings.

I have always mourned the dance of color trapped inside frames of glass. Stained-glass windows that lock rainbow beauty between shards of glass, frozen in place inside stone cathedrals. The light this morning illuminates my own rainbow beauty. I am no longer trapped between panes of glass.

Call me Jacquelyn. I am rooted. I roar. I am rogue. A full spectrum of color.

Say my name. All of it. Every syllable. Unleash notions of he, she, or it. The song of nature is the true tuning fork, the middle C of the soul that harmonizes and aligns us with the vast mystery of being.

Say your name.

◉

We meet most weeks in a glass-lined home tucked into the Sonoran Desert's Santa Catalina Mountains. The private yoga class I teach is not a random group of yoginis. Each one of us was alchemized by lead bullets fired at high speed on a January morning at Safeway. We have been practicing yoga together since 2014 and, on some days, we giggle our way through while on others, especially anniversaries of the shooting or the birthdays of ones who were killed, grief dulls our hearts.

Among the six of us, one lost a son, two were shot, one's husband was wounded, one of us watched, and one of us spent untold time afterward patching together a congressional office while deeply wounded herself by grief.

Gabby joins us when her travel schedule allows. The rest of us try to meet weekly and enjoy each other's company so much that we added a monthly book club to our yoga schedule. A healing space, forged by the profound and myriad ways January 8, 2011, changed each one of us.

We practice yoga in the living room of the home that we have dubbed the Finger Rock Yoga Studio. A haven of wood, glass, rock, and steel nestled in a curve of the Catalinas below Finger Rock, a spindly formation at the top of the mountain with a finger jutting skyward. The house has fourteen-foot ceilings with broad windows facing Finger Rock to the north, Pima Canyon Ridge to the east, and the Santa Rita mountains to the south. The landscape is dotted with long-armed Saguaro, groves of mesquite, and, in the spring, bright yellow brittle bush.

On a recent Wednesday, we chat for at least twenty-five minutes before I make any attempt to begin the class. Gabby had attended a candidate's forum two nights earlier so there was much to discuss.

"Fifteen," Gabby says, rolling her eyes, noting the forum had attracted fifteen candidates that Gabby thought were far too many for a single evening.

I finally begin class with opposite nostril breathing, a deeply calming breath that quiets and settles. We move through side twists, forward folds, Warrior poses, Triangle, and deep core work followed by a long Savasana or final relaxation.

When Gabby moves into Warrior II, she reaches for my arm to find her balance and gently rests her hand on my forearm as she holds the standing pose, right leg bent, left leg extended, right arm extended forward, and left arm behind. A courageous warrior. My heart surges with respect as I stand quietly beside her.

Gabby wants a picture of our group. We line up with a blue yoga mat striped diagonally beneath our feet, our arms looped around each other. Gabby's assistant snaps a picture, and then Gabby requests, "Silly picture."

We stick out tongues, ham for the lens, giggle as the camera clicks.

On a recent Sunday morning, Peter had gone on a long bike ride, and I sit alone enjoying the quiet. A shadow flickers on the living room rug, and I glance out the window. The two Queen Anne palms outside the sliding glass door in our backyard are being danced by a gentle breeze and backlit by the Sun that had just crested Pusch Ridge.

My favorite CD of Laura Sullivan playing on piano Bach's Prelude No. 1 in C Major lilts through the room, and I notice that the shadow dance of fronds on the rug syncs perfectly with the rhythms of Bach. I squint my eyes for a moment and move with the shimmer of music and frond, saturated by the seamless connection of me, sun, ridge, palm, breeze, shadow, and music. The notes of the C major chord are called "root" notes, and they root me in the moment.

Peter and I attended a birthday celebration for Gabby the day before, and images of her, pre-shooting, flash through my brain: riding motorcycles, bicycles, roller blading, climbing mountains, hitching a ride at Mach speed on a jet at Davis-Monthan Air Force Base in Tucson. The bullet to her brain hobbled her speech, paralyzed her right arm and leg, and nearly blinded her. And, she persists.

She continues to climb mountains, jump out of airplanes, and out-core any of us in yoga. She raises millions of dollars through her organization that combats gun violence. Gabby is a ferocious female.

Many years ago, I dreamt of a pioneer woman dressed in calico and bonnet standing by a campfire beside her covered wagon. She plunges an old, well-worn pot with her right hand into the flames. I watch in horror and await her screams, but she is silent. She lifts the pot skyward, now transformed into golden hues. The alchemical fires of transformation.

The alchemy of friendship works its mystery with our yoga group. Each one of us singed by flames of death and grief that could have overpowered us that day in January. Instead, the alchemy of friendship eases our pain, burnishes the ragged edges of our souls.

◉

Lanelle is dead at least four days before she is found. My beloved first cousin born nine months after me. Even though we were bequeathed our mothers' competitive pain, we grew up together, spent many nights at each other's houses, and claimed the elm tree as our own. We shared Sunday School and Sunday suppers, Christmas, Easter, the Fourth of July. Grandma made us matching red-checked taffeta dresses for Christmas one year that we opened on Christmas Eve and modeled for our families, swishing and pirouetting together showing off our lovely new dresses. We graduated together from baby dolls to Barbies, dressing them in clothes Grandma sewed for us—a red strapless gown decorated with lace, Bermuda shorts, and a white satin gown that hugged her curves. Our childhoods intertwined as one.

My sister calls at 7 a.m. on a Wednesday morning in June.

"Have you heard from Nell?"

"No. And it's weird," I tell Gayle. "I texted her on Saturday but never heard back. That's not like her."

"I just got a call from Stella," Gayle tells me, a friend of hers in San Bernardino who is also a friend of Lanelle's. "She hasn't been able to reach Nell either."

Gayle is on her way to her teaching job, so I shift into gear.

I call Lanelle's apartment complex. A recording tells me the office is closed until 9 a.m. but offers an emergency phone number which I call.

"We cannot reach our cousin," I quickly explain to a kind woman who answers. "It's been several days. Can someone please check on her?"

She takes my information and assures me someone will be back in touch.

I call Gayle to let her know and say, "I'm scared."

"Don't jump to conclusions. Let's find out. Maybe her phone is broken."

An hour and a half later, Anais, the manager of Lanelle's apartment complex, calls and gets right to the point.

"She's dead."

I cry out, cell phone glued to my ear, and bolt into our backyard and walk in circles as I talk to Anais.

"Where did you find her?" I ask.

"Near the front door," she tells me. "Maybe a heart attack."

"I hope she died quickly," I say.

"It looks like it. She was propped against the wall just inside the front door. It looked like she just was knocked down."

Lanelle lived alone, had been divorced for years, had a fractious relationship with her mother, and had lost her only child, a son, to drugs. In my heart, I knew she just sat down and said, enough.

Late that afternoon, a gorgeous rainbow arcs across the sky above the ridges of the Catalina Mountains.

"Come look," Peter says as he stands by our bedroom window. I stare into the sky and begin to cry.

"It's Lanelle, it's her!" I tell Peter. "She's in that rainbow of light and color. She had so much pain and now she's a rainbow." The thought gives me comfort.

The next morning, after my 8:30 a.m. yoga class, a young student, new to my class, comes up when class is over.

"Thank you so much," she smiles at me. "That felt so good. It's just what I needed." She pauses a moment. "Can I give you a hug?"

"Of course," I say. We hug. "I'm so glad you liked class. What is your name?"

"Angel," she tells me. I squeal.

"Angel? Are you kidding me? I got hugged by an angel!"

She tilts her head, quizzically, but understands when I explain my dear cousin had just died and a hug from an Angel felt like a message from Lanelle telling me she was fine.

And one more synchronistic flash, this one from Anais, the kind woman at Lanelle's apartment complex who told me Lanelle was dead. She tells me how much they all loved and watched out for Miss Lanelle. A week earlier, Anais says, she helped Lanelle walk to the parking lot to move her car. They walked slowly because of Lanelle's COPD.

"I love it here," she tells Anais, out of the blue. "I love all of you. I'm at peace, I love where I live and I will die here."

Anais teases her, "What if we raise your rent?"

Lanelle answers instantly, "I don't care, I will never leave."

Source gifts us with images, feelings, visions that remind us of our profound connection with all of life and death. Source grants us the ability to see beyond and beneath the narrowness of three-dimensional life. Notice, pay attention. Messages from what people call "the other side" are seen only when we have eyes to see and ears to hear.

Lanelle is color and light. Released from a body that hurt, freed from pain and fear, she is a speck of brilliance amidst the mystery of being. She is grace.

My Dear Mentors,

I offer you my deepest, most profound thanks. You are the ones who led me to still waters and restored my soul. Each of you arriving at different times in my life: as a young child, young woman, middle-aged, and old. You knew, I can only imagine, my soul was ripe and my body eager to receive. You stirred my rogue to life.

Madeline Louise, my mother, you press me close to your side in those early mornings when you whisper the truth of dreams. My vision-queen. You gift me trust and belief in the visions I see in my dreams and in my connection to nature. You teach me respect for the unseen, unknown, the mystery.

Olympia, my guide, you make me stand in the middle of all the loving women and remind me that I hold truth in my teeth. You urge my lips to be silent, to instead dance, sing, sound and let howl the thousand tongues of my heart. You insist I not explain with words but instead experience and release through the power of my body. I dance therefore I am.

Amy, the breath queen, you hold me when I am broken by grief, your soft touch on my back and soft voice fill me with hope, prop me up. You gift me breath as sustenance and glue.

You assure me I have everything necessary, inside my body, to patch myself back together.

Meggan, a gift from the pandemic, the wise Harvard scholar who chose the path of heart over academia. You lead me to words and stories of divine life not found in the Bible. You open my heart to the powerful teachings of Mary Magdalene, Philip, Thomas, Paul, and Thecla. You urge me to drop all pronouns and feel God as Source inside my female body. The font of your wisdom flows off the Zoom screen and into my heart as your gentle voice guides me to imagine, feel, and claim the warm golden honey of The Good. Say it, you urge: I Am The Good.

My rogue thrives as a shapeshifter who deftly slips the bounds of time and space, untethered by manmade segments that tick-tock us through life. The laws of physics clearly state there is no "now" and no "then," but humans love to pretend time is linear, clear-cut, forming safe little cages where we tick off the time until we die. Rogue knows better.

Rogue leads me to bend and slip through before and after and sample and savor what is needed. My body is both a powerful machine and an intuitive creature of imagination and instinct, and I control the levers that message my DNA.

I am the boss of me. This knowledge has both led me to and stemmed from my experience of time and my female body. My body speaks the truth of the fluidity of time and consciousness. I dance each day through a delicious kaleidoscope of sensation and awareness.

The various expressions of time that play me from the inside out: circadian rhythms, monthly blood, the sense of smell and taste that propel one instantly into the past, the mystery of dreams where we glide from past to future to past with an awareness that expands like latex. And not to forget the sacred nine months it takes to spin a human to life inside female bellies.

Crack open your notions of time, sample from all of history, and feel your imagination expand, your instinct find room to breathe, and your intuition step up as your strongest ally. Open to the wisdom of the ages.

⊙

A five-inch scar worms its way vertically up the front of my right thigh ending in the deep fold where leg meets torso. A robot guided a surgeon's knife through my skin, sawed off my femur, and inserted a pink titanium orb. (Pink!).

My skin, puckered, scabbed, and stitched, slowly heals. I feel my body pondering its new man-made-not-god-made ball and socket. As with all new life, this ball and socket arrived in a wash of pain, laid me out, stripped me of autonomy. But today, two and a half weeks in, I feel my body slowly welcoming this intruder like an insect caught in a web of flesh woven by tendons, blood vessels, and nerves.

This body, my body. I write this on Good Friday, the sacred day of dying we all must face if we hope to live a fuller, more deeply sacred life on this Earth. And the dying we also face when who we once were no longer works and old behaviors need to die.

My new hip humbles me into accepting my aging body, but I choose to marvel at my bionic new part that, it turns out, works just as splendidly as the original part that came with me when I was born.

I often tell my yoga students their hips are "the junk drawers of our body." Glutes are the largest muscles in the body. The place we store old stories, emotions, and pain we can't face. The perfect toxic dumping grounds for all we are not ready to process, both ancient and recent.

A cue I always offer when we stand in Mountain pose and, in our mind's eye, scan our bodies from root feet to crown is to release any clenching in the glutes. *Loose glutes,* I invite since it is the place, just like shoulders and jaw, where we unconsciously cling to stress.

A musician friend back east loved to tell her audiences that one's sphincter is directly connected to the voice box. *Loosen up,* she urged her audience. *Loosen your ass hole and it will loosen your voice. Sing!*

The junk drawer of my right hip is wiped clean. I know I will keep stuffing feelings and pain down there, but maybe all that pink titanium will not let it stick. Loose glutes. Hip, hip, hooray.

◉

Bend forward. That's all it takes. Sit, legs stretched forward, and gently ease your chin toward your knees. If you don't quite make it, stack your fists or place a pillow on your lap and rest your head there. Or, stand and move into a full forward fold, bent at the waist, head toward your knees. Hang. Just hang. Neck loose, knees soft, gently nod your head "yes" and "no." Forward folds turn on the calm button of your parasympathetic nervous system. The power of rest, digest. Bow forward, be quiet, and allow the confidence of soul, which blossoms in calm, engulf you.

◉

The iron-hand of perfection for too many years commanded the rudder of my body, steered me from the outside in. It reared its head demanding virginity when I was young and then insisted on expensive clothes, impeccable accessories, and a perfect body as I aged.

Perfection and my ego were best buds. They tag-teamed me in

nagging unison. It felt at times they held a riding crop at my back, snapping, insisting, driving me forward. My soul never gave up even though I tried to smother her with perfection.

I recall the day I go running at lunch from my K Street office to the Washington Monument and back. I return, sweat pouring off me, to my fancy office with its own shower and plop myself into one of the overstuffed chairs, sweat be damned.

My office manager Monica comes in to say hello and I blurt out: "I can't do this anymore." I know my words should not be shared with one of my employees, but the truth would not stay stuffed inside me any longer.

"Are you ok?" Monica asks. She is not quite thirty but both her parents had died a few years apart before she was twenty-five. She understands.

"My soul is worn out," I answer truthfully, staring up at her. "Worn out."

My high-paying corporate job required me to maintain external perfection at all costs. Expensive clothes, work that drained my soul, so many colleagues for whom prestige and power were the designated gods. Smart, always be smart. Marbled, unbloodied perfection froze me in place.

I had yet to learn that yoga, breathwork, and sweat are kryptonite to perfection. Superpowers that melt away addictions to perfection. I would learn that only after bullets and brain cancer derailed my life. But this early recognition, my truth-telling to Monica, begins my slow transformative journey. Worn out by my trek through a shaky world built by individuals overflowing with ego, my soul, which I had pushed deep into the shadows of my being, pokes its messy and imperfect head out and blurts truth to Monica. A confessional moment that ultimately leads me home.

◉

My voice takes center stage when I lead my Monday Zoom class in Yoga Nidra. Always on the full moon or as close to it as possible. Always at the end of a forty-five-minute yoga practice, my voice guides students to lie back on their mats, grab a cushion to support head or knees, use their eye pillow. I am not bragging about my voice but am grateful for its gift of calm. A voice I inherited from my mother.

Chanting, humming, and soothing stimulate the parasympathetic and tone vagal nerves, the largest nerve of our rest-and-digest nervous system that runs from brain to belly.

"Follow my voice. Let it be your anchor." I invite, leading them in their mind's eye, from toes to crown beginning with a focus on breath.

My voice, golden honey, echoes the soft whisper of my mother who comforted me to sleep long ago. It is the voice I use with my adored Benny, our rescue shih tzu, who responds not to my words but to the gentle vibration and tone of love. The voice of soul that burbles from the deepest parts of me.

Nidra calms the central nervous system, invites the imagination to crack open, expand, feel, and dream new ways of being. Nidra works on the body like the finest internal massage, the yummiest bubble bath for the central nervous system. Rest and digest. Rest and digest. Invite your parasympathetic to shine. Add a dollop of full moon energy to the mix and you have a worship service for the imagination and soul.

LIVING FIERCE

Only when it is dark enough can you see the stars.
—Martin Luther King, Jr.

HEY, RACHEL PATTEN, your "Fight Song" comes on today in Safeway as I push my cart through the produce section eyeing the arugula. Your lyrics surge courage through my heart and force my right hand into a fist that simply must be thrust sky-high. With spring mix and spinach as my witnesses, I raise my fist and revel in the surge of power.

I gotta thank you, Rachel. Your words nail it. I feel them heart deep as my very own Rogue Anthem that should be sung daily by every female rogue. All of this on a Tuesday morning at Safeway.

Words do matter. Your words push the on-button for a host of joyful hormones in my body: serotonin, dopamine, endorphins, and oxytocin. All I have to do is let it flow, and cheered on by arugula, I revel in the glory of my rogue-energy who audaciously infuses my life with joy.

◉

Gabby wears a white dress and walks slowly down the left aisle, her step halting, holding on to her husband Mark's hand. The two walk the few steps up to the stage. Mark tells us the documentary we are about to see—*Gabby Giffords Won't Back Down*—might make us cry but they also hope it makes us laugh. The film does both. All the audience, invited for a special screening, have worked or still work for Gabby, rallied to get her elected, support her activism on gun violence, have lost a loved one, have been wounded, or watched the shooting on January 8, 2011.

We are told to arrive early at the Loft Theater in Tucson, Arizona, for security reasons. I am grateful for the security guards in the aisles as the lights go down and the giant screen in front of us fills with light and sound.

Gabby.

I see her on screen, walking through rows of white flowers placed on the mall in Washington, DC, memorializing all who have lost their lives to gun violence. There she is riding her bike on an early morning in Tucson, her face glistening with sweat, telling Mark on a FaceTime call she wishes he were there. The film shows her before the shooting walk sure-footed up the steep steps of the Capitol, speak on the floor of the House of Representatives as a newly elected member and, post-shooting, when she shows up for a critical vote and is met with a standing ovation, the crowd parts as she slowly makes her way through.

I sit in the audience with Peter and fellow former staffers, my eyes glued to the screen, stock still, my every muscle on alert. I know what is coming. Flashes of memory of the shooting reverberate through my brain: looking down at Gabby on the ground, blond hair lit by the Sun, bright red jacket. She's got a pulse, she's got a pulse.

The camera moves to Gabby in the hospital, bullet wound to her head, unconscious, head swathed, breathing tube in place surrounded by doctors, nurses, and Mark, always there by her side. President Obama and First Lady Michelle arrive in Tucson, consoling, meeting with family and friends the very day Gabby, who remained unconscious five days after the shooting, opens her eyes for the first time. *She opened her eyes,* President Obama tells the crowd gathered at a memorial service on January 12, 2011, at the University of Arizona.

She opened her eyes, defying all odds of the brain's response to a bullet blown through its left side. The movie documents Gabby's frustrating efforts to learn to speak and walk again, and her return to public service as a national advocate for gun safety. She never backs down. Instead, she forges forward, a force of nature and courage.

The bullet plants aphasia in her brain, the stealer of words. She is, she reminds us on screen, Gabby, a talker. She has always possessed far more than the gift of gab. An eloquent public speaker, brilliant parser of issues, an artist of articulation. Among my proudest moments as her staffer was sitting in the audience when she delivered a speech I had written. I only wrote a smattering of all the speeches she gave, but I recall this one in particular because it garnered a standing ovation. My words, her presentation, a large room of people on their feet, hands clapping.

Aphasia does not steal all her words. Her speeches today are slower, more heartfelt, each word practiced, memorized, and still she moves audiences to tears, action, standing ovations. The words are in her brain, she tells us on film, but they get stuck there, refusing to make their way into the world.

The exception is music that spills from her naturally. Music lights up multiple parts of the brain, the documentary explains, enables Gabby to sing the music and lyrics of whole songs. Words tucked into melodies do not get stuck.

She is also eloquent in body language through which she speaks legions. No words required. Gabby is a master of touch, smiles, rolled eyes, shrugged shoulders, glares, and glee, the wave of her hand, deep hugs, air kisses, and the love, curiosity, and courage that shine from her every pore. The body language of direct experience, unbound by word-cages, spoken from the whole of her.

Gabby studied in 2021 with three dear friends and her local rabbi for her Bat Mitzvah, a rite requiring extensive reading and reciting that she executed brilliantly. I was honored to attend. And there is this: John Denver's "Country Roads" is among her favorite songs. At a gathering of friends a few years back, several of us stand round the kitchen with Gabby belting out a raucous rendition of "Country Roads." Never missing a word or a beat.

In one of the last scenes of the documentary, Gabby pedals her recumbent bike through her neighborhood singing "Country Roads." A big smile on her face, pedaling, simply pedaling, through a Sonoran afternoon. *Take me home, country roads.*

◉

Female rogue behavior is not encouraged by our world. In truth, culture has long been terrified of female defiance and curiosity. In my own body, rogue-energy is triggered by smell, touch, and images that bring ancient memories of female rogues who have roamed the Earth. I did inherit centuries of female trauma, but I also know, body-deep, that I carry threads of inspiration and courage of female rogues through history.

I have a list I reread on many days to remind me to tend my own rogue-power. The list is heavy on bodily instructions because the powers-that-be, in ancient times and today, believe the easiest way to destroy and deter female rogues is by controlling female bodies. The fact that I need instruction on loving, trusting, and unleashing my female body makes me deeply sad but also deeply hopeful. *I've got this,*

I say to myself. *I know how to claim every inch of embodied female brilliance.* Root, breathe, sweat, pay attention. Let your rogue-flag fly:

- Be voracious in all your hungers. Choose instinct over addiction and live in the place of profound respect for the wonder of your appetites.

- Root yourself in a space of enduring self-love and allow your love of others to flow naturally from that space.

- Educate yourself on the science of your body. Knowledge is power and profound wisdom huddles in your anatomy and physiology. Listen and learn its language.

- Trust direct sensations utterly and completely. Your goose bumps, hemorrhoids, and roiling stomach speak truth.

- Never ignore your dreams—your own creations—spun of fourth-dimensional wisdom that transcend space and time. Write them, live them, trust their guidance.

- Do not believe all written words as truth. Learn the history, context, and motivation for every word written that seeks to define, control, or contain female bodies and sexuality.

- Befriend your clitoris; honor and claim your sexual passion. The most natural expression of being human.

- Know your body's profound connection with nature and source and live, every day, the organic mystery of life and death.

- Question, search for truth, and learn new stories that inspire your DNA to try new expressions of their codes. You can achieve cell-deep transformation.

- Create and follow the lead of your own Rogue Gallery.

- Seek out, pay attention to, and revel in glimmers and gushes of joy and wonder. Every day.

◉

The first time I hear K. D. Lang sing Leonard Cohen's "Hallelujah," I am fifty miles outside of Tucson on I-10 driving to Phoenix for a business meeting. I pop her CD into the car player and her powerful voice engulfs me. Pulse rush, heart beating, what is this song? *Are you listening to this?* I say to myself since no one is in the car with me.

Oh. My. God.

K. D. Lang has been one of my favorites for years. I have seen her in concert at least three times but had never heard her sing "Hallelujah." I pull off at the first exit, park, turn off the car, and hit play. I have to listen again. Fully focused. No engine roar or road noise, just her voice making sweet love to those lyrics.

Mesmerized, transported. I listen to the end of the song and then call my girlfriend who is a huge Leonard Cohen fan.

"Have you heard 'Hallelujah?'" I ask.

"Of course," she says, "one of his best." Why had I never heard it before? I hit play again, close my eyes, bow my head. Levitate.

The song begins slowly in Lang's powerful voice but then crescendos through my body. As it builds, my heart expands to bursting, unties me from chairs and knocks me off pedestals. I have no choice but to join my voice with his and holler loud hallelujahs that echo through my car. A musically induced orgasm. I shimmer and shine.

◉

At my father's memorial service in 1993, Mr. and Mrs. Zimmerman, who had been my softball coaches when I was a kid, show up in the receiving line. I squeal with delight to see them both after more than thirty years. When I hug Mr. Zimmerman, he leans in and whispers in my ear, "You were the best softball player of them all."

His words mean more to me than any accolade or praise I have ever received.

"Really?" I say to him.

"Best I ever coached," he assures me.

Title IX, a Bill of Rights for female athletes, would not become law until 1972. I grew up in the wasteland carved out for girls where physicality was focused on banishing chicken fat and improving one's bust. Today I know a truth I lost sight of in those years. I could have been a contender in several sports. Instead, as so many musical lyrics instructed, I ignored my physical strengths and wasted too much time *wishin' and hopin' and thinkin' and prayin'.*

Two nights ago, I watched the new film *Nyad* starring Annette Bening and Jodie Foster. The long-distance, open-water swimmer Diane Nyad is a master of focus and perseverance. At the age of sixty-four, on her fifth attempt, she swam 111 miles from Havana, Cuba, to Key West. She survived nearly fatal stings by box jellyfish and sucked down so much salt water she threw up repeatedly. She ate every ninety minutes from a tube dangled down from the small boat that carried the team who helped her succeed.

Bening and Foster refused any makeup or touch-ups when they shot the film. They insist the movie focus on the power, complexity, and real faces of older women. I sob as I watch Bening-as-Nyad set foot on dry land in Key West. Her cheeks and lips deformed by stings and salt water. Her dream accomplished. All grit. No glamour.

This morning, I swim my regular sixty minutes of laps. Swimming, yoga, hiking, and free weights keep me strong. Sweat keeps me sane. I'm sure I will never run another marathon or hit a line drive into left field, but I know "wishing and hoping" are not a great life plan. Sweat, however, is always there for me. Every day. I cannot stop aging but I can sweat every day—the joy-juice of my being.

◉

Florence's heavy masculine vibe leaves me gulping from all the celebrations of power and violence exalted in oil, clay, marble, and architecture. Pisa's Square of Miracles in the Piazza del Duomo lights me with joy. Perhaps it is the expanse of green grass on which four key structures are built: the *duomo* or cathedral; a separate leaning bell tower, the most famous structure in Pisa; a baptistery; and a *composanto* or cemetery. Each structure pays homage to the human life cycle.

"All phases of human lives are honored in the Square of Miracles," our guide tells us. "Baptism, rituals of marriage and faith and death are on equal ground in the Piazza."

We wander the grassy expanse, take the requisite snapshot of each of us leaning toward the tower of Pisa to set it straight. The sky is bright blue, the temperature perfect, the crowds light.

"There is a special surprise for you in the baptistery," our guide tells us. Construction of Pisa's baptistery, the largest one in Italy, began in the 1100s and was completed in the 1300s. It is circular, Romanesque on top and Gothic below, and resembles the Capitol in Washington, DC, if you shaved off the dome and plopped it on solid ground. The interior features an ornate pulpit that rises high above the masses that is decorated with a nude Hercules sculpted somewhere close to 1260 CE.

The surprise our guide promises is the gift of sound. Once we are all inside, they close the doors and a young man walks to one side of the rounded interior, cups his hands around his mouth, and begins to chant into the domed ceiling. His singular voice reverberates from ceiling to floor as if a whole choir has joined his song.

We stand quietly enveloped by sound. I imagine all the babies held in parental arms awaiting holy waters on their head. I can hear ancient voices chanting through the centuries proclaiming new life, saying "I do," affirming faith. Voices that will move from baptistry to *duomo* to final rest in the cemetery as the bell tower tolls the passing years, honoring all our human beginnings and endings.

I am awed not panicked by the architectural tributes to and respect for all aspects of human life: female, male, birth, death, mystery, ritual, elation, grief, rogue, and holy woman. Domed together as one within the continuum of sound.

◉

Rain falls on our desert town all day long on December 22. A gentle soaking winter rain that sates the cacti for months to come. The next morning, I stare up at snow-capped Catalina Mountains and breathe in the fragrance of desert-after-rain: squeaky-clean with a bite of creosote. That night, we continue our annual tradition of watching *A Christmas Story,* the movie that takes place in the 1950s and features Ralphie who is desperate for Santa to bring him an official Red Ryder, carbine action, two hundred–shot, range model air rifle.

The movie oozes nostalgia, and as I breathe in the glory of our rain-soaked valley, I understand why Ralphie did not draw me in as he usually does each year. Nostalgia exerts a powerful pull on human hearts, yanking them backward in time to the good old days. Nostalgia is memory buffed and polished until it glimmers like gold, while my rogue-journeys have led me through mud, shit, half-truths, and shame.

Nostalgia suffocates all things rogue. Why bother to blaze a different path forward when the good old days lure you into complacency? I have come to know my rogue very well. She is unbound by all segments of time whether minutes, hours, or centuries. She has clawed her way out of creeds and dogma, dragged healthy, robust, juicy female sexuality out of the dust bins of history, and knows bone-deep that divisions by gender are being eroded by the slow and steady drip of fluidity.

Nostalgia fills me with sepia-tinted memories of Santa Claus, Christmas lights, the soft cheek of my grandmother and mom and dad's adoration of all things Christmas. A heaping platter of warm-fuzzy *selective* memory that edits out angst and grief.

Nostalgia is the fairy tale.

As I stare up at the mountain, I know my body and DNA have joined forces to open my eyes and ears to new ways of feeling and being in the world. I can now recall Christmas past without longing, and am simply grateful for Christmas present that gifts me winter rain topped with a dollop of creosote. No official Red Ryder air rifles required.

◉

The booklet my mother gives me so many years earlier about becoming a young woman focuses on my reproductive system. The little booklet carries a powerful implicit message: The most important part of your body is reproduction. Why does no one inspire me to know the innate strength, intuition, and instinct of my female body? Why aren't I told I hold all the levers of ignition in my hands? Why no word on my clitoris? Why no heads-up about my vagal nerves?

Wanna dance with passion? Head toward your clitoris. Need yourself some calm? Move your fingers in gentle massaging circles along the vagal nerves that travel down both sides of your neck, close to the surface. The vagal is the main nerve of the parasympathetic nervous system, which calms the body. The conduit out of flight or fight and into the world of rest and digest. It hungers to be toned, massaged, engaged.

Vagal toning does not require expensive yoga clothes, $100 yoga mats, instructors, or certification. Deep breathing, gentle massage, long side-body stretches, and forward folds turn on your calm. The vagal nerve is central to health and well-being. A mighty connection between brain and belly where the two talk regularly: brain to belly and belly to brain. Each one fully aware of the power of the other and eager to work as powerful partners. Deep-belly knowing and gut instinct never lie.

We do not need one more diagram of ovaries and fallopian tubes but could benefit from diagrams of the vagal nerves. Follow its lead as it makes its way from the brain, down both sides of the neck, along the side body, and into the belly. Stroke it, talk to it, tone and stimulate it every day.

Self-care is the best way to inspire your DNA to try new ways of living. Show up on behalf of your body, your hungers, your ability to digest and release. Your DNA will take note. No more negative body-talk you learned as a child that is reinforced by advertising in all forms of media. Enough with emotional baggage that has saddled female hunger for centuries. Bend forward, breathe deeply, ignite the superpower of your vagal nerves.

You be the boss.

◉

He comes in a dream that lasts all night. Tall and thin, an angular nose, attired in a full-dress military uniform. His presence, not appearance, attract, root, and calm me. *I love you,* I whisper to him and he looks up, startled. He does not parrot back my words but stares deep into my eyes. He is there to strengthen, not rescue. *I care deeply about you,* he whispers, and I know his vow comes from a place of abiding love. We are standing side-by-side, fully dressed. Our lips never touch. My dream ends not with a passionate embrace but with the profound connection of resonating souls. The thousand tongues of his heart, spoken through his gaze, mesh with the thousand tongues of my heart. My soul mate. He will never abandon me.

The day before my dream, I slouch on the couch in despair. A crick in my neck, my knee aching. I feel old, useless, worn out. Inert and despairing.

"Are you okay?" Peter asks.

"I just don't have any energy," I tell him.

It is day three of hard freezes in my beloved Sonoran Desert. Frozen nights and chill, windy days pen me in. *This is nuts,* I say to myself as I shake myself off the couch, lace up my tennis shoes, and go into our backyard. It is about two in the afternoon, warm enough, and I begin walking in circles, round and round our patio. I decide to add a smile.

"Did you know," I asked Peter a few days earlier, "if you fake smile your body doesn't know it's fake. It still cranks up endorphins."

I walk in circles and fake smile for a good twenty minutes, hoping no neighbors notice my head bobbing round and round, visible just above the brick wall. Grinning like an idiot, refreshing my body and soul with happy hormones.

We can alter our moods with everyday tweaks: hug a family member and oxytocin fires; savor a juicy peach and feel the dopamine; remind yourself to laugh or go for a walk and endorphins flood your body; take a few moments to close your eyes, listen to your breath, and breathe belly-deep to release serotonin. Or simply walk in circles around your backyard and fake smile. There's a whole lotta happy juice, the favorite drink of your rogue, inside your body.

Going rogue can feel lonely. My incessant hankering for truth and change feels like it sets me apart from family and friends. Why can't I simply sink into nostalgia? Cement myself in the good old days? Why not keep repeating old habits that, even if not good for me, are known and comfortable? Why not dull my soul and narrow my Self?

The simple truth is that the eyes of all those females trapped in oil and clay in the Uffizi do not want me mired in inertia. They latched on and are here to stay. Another truth: I don't want them to release me, and I cannot let them down.

The female eyes reawakened my rogue: a surging current, body-deep, of curiosity, indignance, and a total inability to settle for what feels like an ill-fitting suit created by culture with pants too tight, arms too short, a crotch that cuts deep. Rogue wants, most of all, for me to love all of who I am, be everything I love best, and rally other females to change the world, one female body at a time.

The prince in my dreams convinces me I am on the right path. He would not have arrived years ago when my ego was in charge. This prince personifies full-hearted masculinity unbound by conquer and control. He could only have shown up when my powerful female energy and soul had found their ground. The two exist as essential complements to one another.

The images and sensations my prince inspires in me mix and mingle DNA-deep and shift who I am in the world. He fills my body with wonder and strength and drains away sensations of trauma and anxiety, both ancient and familial.

◉

A coyote crosses the street in front of my car as I drive home from the grocery store. Not so close I have to slam on my brakes but close enough I am gifted a close-up view of his sleek form as he dashes across and then deftly scales, with nary a pause, a 110-degree, twenty-five-foot manmade rock wall built to stem erosion. He glides with ease up and over the steep embankment before vanishing into a stretch of raw desert.

Not unlike the bobcat who lands in our backyard years earlier, coyote stirs my wild juices. A deep-body thrumming similar to the panic attacks that roiled me at Target and in the Uffizi, but this one churns with awe at coyote's wild spirit.

Instead of anxiety, I am filled with wonder, a lightness of being, the taste of freedom to roam large in the world. The intensity of my response, just like my Uffizi experience, convinces me wildness is a state of being that my DNA once knew and still remembers.

Why isn't there a named syndrome to capture a wonder-attack? PTSD is well researched and widely known. Why not Post Ecstatic Wonder Syndrome, also called PEWS, for the soul where the body, unlike on hard church pews, sings its hallelujahs with goose bumps and happy hormones? My body convinces me that wonder, awe, and mystery live in my DNA just like ancient trauma and can be stirred to life with new experiences.

After my coyote sighting, I eagerly go into our backyard for my favorite pay-attention ritual: rooting both feet on the patio and staring up at my mountain buddies as tingling sensations of wonder and awe sparkle through me. I am filled to brimming with the profound sense of mysterious connection with all of nature. I wiggle fingers and toes, let the joy, like music, entice my body into a happy dance, arms flailing, hips wiggling, a goofy dance of joy.

My rogue, I am certain, takes her orders from the depths of my body and soul. I like to imagine my rogue as my soul-soup chef who takes the stock DNA ingredients I was born with that were seasoned by my early upbringing and stirs them into new concoctions of being. Rogue knows my body is science, nature, imagination, and instinct and blends all of me into a beautiful stew that nourishes my shaky little ego.

I see my rogue wearing a tall white toque and wielding a large wooden spoon that cuts through time. She strengthens the broth of me with coyote and bobcat bones, and then seasons and simmers my DNA into a glorious stew of body, soul, imagination, dreams, and instinct.

Listen to rogue-rumblings from the depths of your body. Trust. Live the tastes your tongue likes best. Bring to full boil your delicious, bodacious, courageous self. Climb out of manmade boxes, tromp over manmade lines in the sand, discard binary boxes of confinement.

Claim the stars.

The female eyes of the ancients demand: *Be all that we could never be.* They lived narrowed and confined lives and proclaim how desperately today's world needs fully embodied females. In sheer numbers, females comprise half the population of the world, but are ascribed nowhere close to half the power. We walk the Earth in bodies regulated by others. We pray in too many churches where females are prohibited to lead. We obediently dislike our own bodies, ignore our own hungers, and are mired in fear over how to live passionately in a dangerous world.

The warnings of the Uffizi females do not fall on deaf ears. They open my eyes and ears. They stir my rogue back to life and hurry me up with their urgent pleas to release them by spreading the word. They demand my fierce attention to my rogue-energy.

May we all cook up new ways of being female in our world in bodies cleansed of fear and anxiety, dancing with joy and hope. May we all learn the language of our bodies and follow rogue curiosity where it leads. Let rogue erase dichotomies, either-or, virgin-whore, and lead us to living whole and healthy.

◉

Bonnie Raitt is a singer-songwriter-guitarist who won a Lifetime Achievement Award at the 2022 Grammy's. Her music is inspired by blues, jazz, and so much more. I have been to her live concerts at least five times. As an article in *The Guardian* noted, "Her unquestionable gift is the way she can interpret and reimagine music intuitively, motivated by a desire to find stories." Raitt provides an even better take on how she makes her music. She credits "someone" for the quote that she says describes her music-making process: "You can't change the noodle, but you can change the sauce."

I stumble on Bonnie's quote one morning as I sit on the toilet thumbing through my Facebook feed. There she is with the unsourced, borrowed quote:

You can't change the noodle, but you can change the sauce.

The quote hits me like a splash of cold water. *She's talking about rogue,* I say to myself. *She is all about rogue.*

We can't change the DNA we are born with, but we can create our own spicy sauce of a life with the ingredients that come to us through our imaginations, dream images, intuition, sweat, and breath. We can concoct, using the DNA we are born with, the sauciest, sexiest, steamiest, most sacred lives imaginable. We are the creators.

"Nick of Time" is among Bonnie's greatest hits. She writes of the hard choices we face and how precious life is when "there's less of it to waste." She urges us to live fiercely.

Civilization has little time to waste to clean up its act. If the female half of the world's population remains cemented into worrying about external appearance instead of living the truth and power of female creation, intuition, instinct, and dreams, the patriarchy's obsession with conquer and control will continue. We are all screwed.

The noodle that is life on this Earth needs no more canned Chef Boyardee spaghetti sauce (note the "boy" at the heart of this sauce) and a whole lot more secret sacred sauce spun from female imagination and experience. Rogue assures us we hold the power and tools of change inside our mysterious and wondrous female bodies. Go rouge. Right now. Fiercely. In the nick of time.

ACKNOWLEDGMENTS

A VERY SPECIAL THANK YOU to all of the female statues and images in Florence's Uffizi Galleries whose eyes latched onto my body and refused to let go until I wrote their story. And to my mother, who, despite her young death at 58, bequeathed me a lifelong belief and trust in the brilliance of my dreams. She taught me the language of dreams, the truth of imagination and to listen closely and act on messages that resonate deeply through my body as happened when all the eyes bored into me.

This book has lived through several iterations and a special thanks to my writing buddies who stuck with me through them all: Deanne Stone, Linda Tuthill, Joan Cicak, Emily Nottingham, Pam Simon, Karen Christensen and Susan Tarrance.

Thanks also to the dear souls who demonstrated their skills as brilliant readers and ardent supporters: my sister Gayle Jackson Hastings, Peggy Mullaney, Stephanie Healy, Donna Mabry, Jennifer Kinsey, Susan Fifer Canby, Mary Beth Ginter and Dan Docks, Joni Jones, Nancy Barber, Sheri Scavo, Twyla Salaiz, Ellen McDonnell, and Jennifer Carnes. And a special thanks to my most trusted reader: my husband Peter Michaels.

A grateful nod to the team at She Writes Press, especially Brooke

Warner, Shannon Green, and Lauren Wise. And to my publicity team at Wildbound PR including Julia and Jared Drake.

Writing, publishing, and selling books absolutely takes a village. I am forever humbled and grateful to my village of rogues who made this book come true.

ABOUT THE AUTHOR

Photo credit: Rachel Marie Castillo

JACQUELYN L. JACKSON is a writer, yoga instructor and clinical social worker whose work and practice have focused on claiming the full power and health of life in a female body. Her journalism and essays have appeared in a range of publications including the *Boston Globe* and *Los Angeles Times* and have been aired on National Public Radio. She lives with her husband Peter in the Sonoran Desert city of Tucson, Arizona.

Looking for your next great read?

We can help!

Visit www.shewritespress.com/next-read
or scan the QR code below for a list
of our recommended titles.

She Writes Press is an award-winning
independent publishing company founded to
serve women writers everywhere.